MY WAR

& WELCOME TO IT

TOM COPELAND

SUNBURY
PRESS

Mechanicsburg, PA USA

Published by Sunbury Press, Inc.
Mechanicsburg, Pennsylvania

SUNBURY
P R E S S

www.sunburypress.com

For information about special discounts for bulk purchases, please contact Sunbury Press Orders Dept. at (855) 338-8359 or orders@sunburypress.com.

To request one of our authors for speaking engagements or book signings, please contact Sunbury Press Publicity Dept. at publicity@sunburypress.com.

ISBN: 978-1-62006-329-3 (Trade paperback)

Library of Congress Control Number: 2019948985

FIRST SUNBURY PRESS EDITION: August 2019

Product of the United States of America
0 1 1 2 3 5 8 13 21 34 55

Set in Bookman Old Style
Designed by Crystal Devine
Cover by Lawrence Knorr
Edited by Lawrence Knorr

Continue the Enlightenment!

CONTENTS

PREFACE

For the past twenty years, something inside me has wanted out. It keeps telling me I should write a book, I should let people know what this thing is about. That something has not told me what it is or why people should know about it, it just wants out. When talking to other Vietnam veterans I get the same feeling from them. Although they don't always say it, you can tell by listening to them that something needs to be said. Something needs to be set free.

My hope in writing this book is that whatever it is inside me, and people like me, will come out, and in the process, set us all free. In thinking about this book, I keep looking for a beginning and an end. The beginning, I have decided, must start somewhere in my years as a teenager growing up in New Mexico. Those were the happy, carefree years before the war before I was aged beyond my years, before I became an old man before my time. The ending will be when this thing inside me is out and I am free. When I can look at the Vietnam Veterans Memorial Wall and not feel suddenly cold and far away. When I can listen to the song "Old Hippie" and not cry when I hear the passage;

> *"He was sure back in the sixties; that everyone was hip*
> *till they sent him off to Vietnam; on his senior trip.*
> *They forced him to become a man; while he was still a boy.*
> *Behind every wave of tragedy, he waited for the joy."*

("Old Hippie," written by David Bellamy, 1985)

I think I shall miss this thing because it has been my constant companion for more than twenty-seven years. I believe whatever it is inside me, has helped mold me into the person I am today. I also believe by facing it and discussing it, it can help me settle into the later years of my life. This thing inside me wants out, and it needs out. I only hope that by freeing it I bring something beneficial into my life and the lives of those I love, and not lose something. I also hope that by reading this book other people like me can benefit. I hope this is not another attempt to get it out, that results in burying it deeper.

CHAPTER 1

WHERE DO I BEGIN

To truly understand my feelings and personal torment about my time in Vietnam, it is important to understand my roots—those things that shaped my life, and my very being, prior to the extreme changes experienced during my tour of duty in Vietnam.

I was born in Levelland, Texas on April 6, 1947. My dad worked in the oil fields of west Texas and eastern New Mexico and my mom spent most of her years making a home and caring for four kids and a husband. We were a close family and some of my fondest memories are of the large family gatherings with grandparents, aunts, uncles, and cousins. The family spent holidays and vacations together and often went on hunting, fishing and camping trips. When I was four years old we moved from Levelland to Hobbs, New Mexico. I started school in Hobbs and when I was in the third grade we moved to Monument, New Mexico. Monument is a very small community located in the southeastern corner of the state. The primary industries in the area are ranching, dryland farming, and petroleum. Living in the desert was a far cry from surviving in the jungles of Vietnam, but in some instances, living in the desert helped prepare me mentally for what I would experience in Vietnam. My experiences in the desert started the development of life skills I would need during my tour in Vietnam.

My strongest remembrances of the desert are the smells and the sounds. The feel of the hot dry air during the day, and the cool desert air at night. Senses that were developed in every young man growing up and roaming across the pastures and rangelands of southeastern New Mexico. The clean clear air was filled with the aroma of sagebrush and desert flowers and with occasional whiffs of the smells of crude oil and sour gas.

On clear nights, which were most of the time, I could see for miles across the desert. The distant towns and cities cast a halo of light onto the southwestern sky. The expanses of darkness between the towns were dotted with the flames of burning petroleum flares and the lights on oil well drilling platforms. The light of a million stars punctuated the darkness of the southwestern sky. The towns, the flares, and the oilrigs seemed so close, but so far away. I can remember looking at the stars and thinking they were so close you could reach out and touch them. I wondered how many people on earth were looking at the same stars I was looking at, a thought that would come again and again during my service in Vietnam. The sounds of the desert are like nowhere else on earth I have ever been. I often walked through the expanses of the rangeland that surrounded our home, hunting rabbits with my .22-caliber rifle. To survive in the desert, it was important to not only depend on your sense of sight, but also on your sense of sound and smell. I developed the ability to recognize bugs and reptiles by the sounds they made and the smells they gave off. To distinguish the difference in the sounds of a grasshopper flying and the warning sounds of rattlesnakes. Off in the distance, you could hear oil well pumpjacks busily and sporadically pumping crude oil from the wells and into pipelines to be carried miles away for processing. The lazy turning of the windmills pumping water from far beneath the desert floor to support life where nature had not intended it to be.

Scouting was a big activity for all of us in our younger years. Although the local leaders tried to put on a good program, there were just not enough qualified men in the community to support a top-notch Scouting program. My dad, who had never participated in Scouting as a youngster, was always there and always willing to help. Despite requests from the Boy Scout troop to become a trained leader, my dad refused to take the courses. He didn't want to do all that book learning; he just wanted to share his experiences of growing up in the great outdoors. Although he couldn't teach us everything we needed to know to get our merit badges, he could show us how to fish and hunt, build cooking fires, and provide for ourselves in the wilderness. And most importantly, my dad showed the Scouts how to have a good time together in the wilderness.

My friends and I would often make overnight outings into the rangelands, pasturelands, and sand dunes and set up campsites for a night or two. We would usually take enough food to hold us over, but, occasionally we killed rabbits to cook over the open fire. On most occasions, we would sit by the fire telling stories and just enjoy being young bucks growing up in the wilds of New Mexico. On other occasions, we would cook our meal and wait for nightfall so we could start the games. Sometimes we would choose sides and play a game of group hide and seek. The object was to find all the members of the opposing team without having all your members found. Some guys were good at hiding, and others were good at finding. My strong point was hiding. I would often lie between sagebrush plants or tucked under a mesquite bush while the other team members walked within inches of me. I could hear them whispering and could have sworn they could hear my heart pounding in my chest. I would lie very still until they passed, and then, turn my head very slowly to see if they were out of sight. Once they were gone I would carefully low crawl to a new hiding spot. If I ever had a "God-given talent" it was the ability to hide in plain sight. In Advanced Infantry Training at Fort Polk, Louisiana, I had a Drill Instructor come close to stepping on me during a field exercise. When I moved to avoid being stepped on, it scared the shit out of him and got me an ass chewing.

CHAPTER 2

A BOY AND HIS GUN

Much of my youth was spent roaming and hunting in the desert of New Mexico or on weekend fishing trips to the Pecos River with my dad and my friends.

After school, my friends and I would use our lunch money to buy a box of shells for our .22-caliber rifles and walk across the pastures hunting rabbits. We developed our marksmanship skills by shooting at lizards, bugs, cow shit, and mesquite bush limbs. We would occasionally get a spoon from the kitchen and take turns shooting at it until nothing was left. The big challenge was to find a windmill with most of the blades missing and try to hit a blade while it was rotating. Nothing was safe when we were armed. Cans, fence posts, water towers, and rural mailboxes were all fair game. The rabbits and small game were often safer than the inanimate objects. Although we did our part to reduce the population of rabbits and snakes in the area, we did not always hit what we were shooting at.

In the fall we went deer hunting in the mountains around Capitan and Ruidoso, New Mexico. During the early years, my dad would buy a hunting license for me but would only let me hold the rifle while he took a "leak" in the woods. I was only allowed to shoot the big guns for target practice. The reason for buying a hunting license was to allow dad to bring out two deer, which did not always work. My dad was one hell of

4

an outdoorsman, but, his luck at hunting was subject to the same things every other hunter faced, being in the right place at the right time. Some years he shot more than his share of deer and several people in the camp would go home happy. Other years he returned home empty-handed. You could bet on those years he bagged a deer and put my deer tag on it, I got to do lots of target practice in the woods before we brought the deer out past the New Mexico Fish and Game Department's checkpoints.

As I got older, I was allowed to carry a rifle. My favorite was the Winchester Model 94, saddle gun. I dearly loved that rifle. When I carried that rifle all my cowboy heroes were right there with me.

One year, dad had gone hunting by himself during the first week of hunting season. He came home empty handed so he and I planned a one-day trip on a Saturday. We got up very early and headed for the mountains. The hunting area was about a three-hour drive from home so we got there just after the sun came up. We started walking down the valley between two very steep mountain ridges and had only walked about fifteen to twenty minutes when Dad spotted the most magnificent buck. He had the largest rack of any deer I had ever seen on any deer, living or dead. My dad told me I could have this one but to wait until he told me to shoot. We both took careful aim and he gave me the word. I took a deep breath and carefully squeezed the trigger. It seemed like it was taking forever to move the trigger into the release position so against all my training, I gave it a quick jerk. The rifle dipped down slightly, the shell exploded and the bullet hit the rocks just under the deer's belly. I guess my dad knew I would screw-up my first shot and he was ready. As the deer lurched forward he squeezed off a round and the deer stumbled to the ground. He opened the bolt action to put in another shell and the rifle jammed. While he was clearing the jam, the deer got up and started moving along the ridge. I opened up with the Winchester Model 94. Although it was a lever action rifle, when the buck fever kicked in, I managed to get off several rounds

Tom and Gene Copeland, deer hunt, 1960

shooting the hell out of all matter of rocks and trees, but, not coming close to the deer. By the time dad got his rifle cleared and got me settled down the deer was out of sight. We knew dad had wounded it and we set out to track it. When we last saw the buck, he was moving along the ridge back up into the mountains. Dad took the high ground and I proceeded to walk along the valley. As I walked along I tried to settle myself down and chastised myself for getting buck fever. I carefully searched each tree and bush for signs of the deer. I waited to hear Dad's rifle fire again but everything was quiet. Then I heard dad yell, "I got the bastard." I couldn't tell where his voice was coming from so I called out to him. He responded that he was under the tall dead tree. From my vantage point, I could see several dead trees in the direction his voice was coming from. I picked the one I thought the sound came from and started up the mountain. As I walked up, dad was busy gutting the deer and I noticed he was shaking. I asked if he was OK, and he said that big buck had just scared the shit out of him. When he found the deer, he was lying still under the tree with his eyes closed. Dad placed his rifle against a tree and pulled out his hunting knife. As he got close to the buck, it opened its eyes and started to get up. Rather than take a chance of losing the buck again by going back for his rifle, dad went for the deer's throat with his knife. Just as he grabbed the buck's head he started to rise and dad knew he was about to become one of those hunting stories that start out, "Did you hear about that poor dumb bastard who tried to kill a deer with a hunting knife . . ." We had both witnessed what a deer could do to a man a few years earlier when a man in the camp next to ours jumped out of his tree perch and roped a big buck without shooting it first. The buck won!

Dad gutted out the deer and we started the long trek back to the car carrying our prize. An eleven-point Colorado mule deer. We got back to the car, tied the deer on, and were on our way back home by 10:00 A.M.

CHAPTER 3

PECOS TOM

It was during elementary school that I first heard the stories about Pecos Bill. Pecos Bill was a young boy who fell off a covered wagon while it was crossing the Pecos River. Bill came from a large family so it was several days before he was missed. Once it was discovered that he was missing they never went back to look for him figuring the animals had already eaten him. Bill was taken in by a pack of wolves and raised as one of their own. He spent the rest of his life carving out a living on the banks of the Pecos River. Although I didn't fall off a wagon, and I wasn't raised by wolves, I did spend a considerable amount of time on the Pecos River creating and living my own stories.

While I was growing up, my family spent vacations on lakes and rivers, fishing and swimming. We had large family gatherings, often camping at the water's edge. My grandparents, aunts, and uncles would all be there. Most of the time, we camped in tents or under the open sky. Occasionally we would borrow, or rent a cabin and the kids usually ended up on the living room floor or on the porch, sleeping on cots and pallets. My favorite place was on a cot placed next to the campfire where I would drift off to sleep staring at the flames or gazing at the stars.

In high school, my trips to the Pecos River changed drastically. My friends and I would head for the river on

Bill, Tom, Dorothy, & Thelma Copeland, fishing trip, 1952

Saturday morning and not come home until late Sunday evening. We would fish for an hour or so and then get into the water and play.

Fishing was a big part of my life during my youth and remains so today. Many times during my tour in Vietnam, I had the urge to throw a line into the small holes of water that served as bathing spots for the Vietnamese. Sometimes we would pass a water hole and see the kids fishing with a piece of string tied onto a bamboo stick. In some respect, it reminded me of my times on the water only a few years earlier. My water holes were larger and the equipment was better, but, I am sure these boys were feeling the same emotions and pleasure I experienced before I became so old and tired.

I was really excited about my first fishing trip after Vietnam but, for some reason, it just wasn't the same. Somehow the magic and sheer pleasure were replaced with restlessness. It would be several years after getting out of the Army before I could relax and find peace and calm in the great outdoors again.

CHAPTER 4

SCHOOL DAYS

During my years in school, I was a less than average student. In elementary school, I enjoyed school and showed some real promise, but as time passed I began to lose interest in school. Since I never thought I was smart enough to get a scholarship to college, and I didn't think my parents had enough money to get me there, I didn't see the point in busting my ass in high school. My grades eroded to just barely passing and sometimes below, which was all I needed to graduate. I had fun in high school but I didn't break any academic records. If it hadn't been for one particular teacher, I may not have graduated with the rest of my class. Mrs. Harrod put some of the drive back into me and scared the shit out of me at the same time. I will always be indebted to her for turning me around and making me see the importance of education. I had three teachers during my twelve years in the public school system who made a lasting impression in my life.

First, there was Mrs. Cates, in the third grade, who allowed me the freedom to explore in the classroom. Every day she read a story to the class as we took turns standing behind her brushing her hair. I don't know how that tradition got started but it was something that all her students looked forward to, even the bullies and the tough guys. Mrs. Cates taught us more than just what was on the lesson plan. She taught us to explore the things that we were really interested in and to develop those areas of interest. She gave us time to realize who we were and to get comfortable with that. She taught us to care for each other and for ourselves. Looking back now, I think she was twenty to thirty years ahead of her time with her classroom philosophy. She didn't care how you learned your lessons, she only cared that you learned them, and got some value out of attending her class.

In junior high school, there was Mrs. Curry. She was the first tough woman teacher I ever met. She never let on that she was afraid of anything or anybody. I saw her take down some of the toughest guys in school with just the tone of her voice. She never laid a hand on anyone during the years I knew her, but, she kept everyone in her class in line. Since my dad worked with and sometimes fished with, her husband, I stayed in line in her class. Her homework assignments got done first and I caused very little trouble in her classroom. Although she was tough, she was always fair and open to lending a hand when asked to do so. I took that characteristic from her and have tried to use it as well as she did.

Then in high school came Mrs. Harrod, nicknamed "Horrid Harrod." This was my teacher from hell! She probably did more for me than any single person, other than my own parents. Mrs. Harrod had graduated from high school at the age of sixteen and entered college. She was teaching College English at the age of nineteen. She taught College English for thirty-three years and retired. After a year in retirement, she moved to Hobbs to temporarily fill a position in the English Department. This woman was no more than five feet tall and probably weighed less than one hundred pounds. In her own mind, she could have been a first-string player for any professional football team. Her motto was "the bigger they are, the harder they fall", and the more enjoyment she got out of knocking them down.

The first day of class she made it a point to let us know who she was, what she expected from each of us and what we could expect from her. During the first week of class, she caught me playing around during a reading session. She walked up behind me, grabbed the hair on the nap of my neck, raised me slowly about two inches above my chair and told me she was going to do a bear dance on the back of my neck. I didn't know what the hell a bear dance was, but, I was sure I didn't want to find out. She ran the classroom with military precision, she was in charge and everyone knew it. Looking back now, her tactic was to go after the biggest guys in the room and get their undivided attention and respect. At six-feet two-inches, I was one of the prime targets. After that, the rest of the class was putty in her hands. Above all, she was very fair and showed a genuine concern for the students in her class. She organized study sessions at her home after school to help anyone needing extra help. She was demanding but fair and sensitive.

One of our assignments during the year was to memorize and recite a section of the Prologue to Chaucer's Canterbury Tales. We had to memorize and recite the assignment in Middle English. I worked hard to memorize the passage because I wanted to show Horrid Harrod that I could do it. I spent weeks outside our home practicing the passage because I was too embarrassed to have anyone in the family hear me talking in Middle English. When it came time to recite the assignment in class I could not do it. When I refused to stand in front of the class Mrs. Harrod saw that something was bothering me and requested to see me before school the next morning. When we met I told her that I knew the assignment but I could not recite it in front of the class. She asked if I would mind reciting it to her and I let it out.

> *"Whan that Aprill with it shoures sote*
> *The droghte of Marche hath perced to the rote,*
> *And bathed every veyne in swich licour*
> *Of which vertu engendred is the flour: . . ."*

> ("The Prologue" from *The Canterbury Tales*, by
>   Geoffrey Chaucer)

And so on. When I finished she praised me for what I had done and gave me full credit for the assignment. She said it was so nicely done she wanted me to do it in front of the entire class, and she would give me extra credit for doing it. Although I really needed all the credit I could get, I declined. She told me she understood and that it was OK. I had never been given a break like that by any teacher before. Although I felt like a bit of a failure, because I couldn't do it in front of the class, Mrs. Harrod said she understood and wouldn't ask me to do anything that would make me uncomfortable. She had all the qualities of a true leader and she passed some of it on to me and anyone else lucky enough to have been taught by her. More than any other teacher, Mrs. Harrod was responsible for helping me get my act together and graduate from high school. She taught me those lessons in true leadership that would serve me well, not only in Vietnam but throughout my working career.

GREEN'S
HOBBS, N. MEX.
Tom, high school graduation, 1965

I was active in sports in junior high school but as I moved into high school I dropped out of sports and became active in the band. Those memories made in the band have lasted a lifetime. The band did a lot of traveling to out of town football games. If the team was playing within a two-hour drive from the school, the band went along. We performed a half time show and played spirited fight songs during the games. In my senior year of high school, I joined a Country and Western band. We first started out just playing for our own enjoyment, then someone got us a job. We liked playing for dances so much we decided to try to get a job every other weekend. That lasted for about three months and we found ourselves playing every weekend and sometimes twice on the weekend. We

Practice session, 1965

began to travel around the southeastern corner of New Mexico and into the panhandle area of Texas. When I left the band to move to Indiana, one of the members was talking about getting a bus and going on the road. Although it sounded exciting, I elected to move to Indiana instead. That move was the end of my music career.

It was in high school that I first heard about Vietnam. I didn't really understand the significance of what I was hearing and didn't give it much thought. It was just world news stuff that never effects people in small towns in New Mexico. Besides, we were having too much fun running wild across the countryside and drinking beer to worry about a war in a place we had never heard of.

CHAPTER 5

GO EAST YOUNG MAN

After graduating from high school in May 1965, I worked several jobs around my home. I tried my hand at ranching, farming, and oil field construction, none of which were new experiences for me and none of which I cared to do.

The farming part was the worst. The soil in the desert is so dry, to grow crops, the land must be watered. Some people choose to install large sprinkler systems that spray water out over the crops, while others choose to deliver water to their crops using the less costly irrigation methods. In irrigation, ditches are dug along the sides of the fields and small trenches are dug between the rows of crops. The ditches are flooded and the water is siphoned from the ditches into the trenches. The ditches and trenches had to be cleaned out on a regular basis. One of my jobs was to walk along the ditches and trenches with a shovel and dig out the obstructions to keep the water flowing properly. It was, at times, very awkward to stand beside the trenches, between the plants and dig out the trenches without stepping on any of the plants. This job was not what I was looking for, and after a week or two, I was looking again. The next job was working at Oilfield Construction.

A construction company had been contracted to build a pumping station a few miles from my house. Two of my buddies and I managed to get ourselves hired by the construction company. Our first job was to clean out ditches that were being dug for concrete footing for a building. The ditch was about eighteen inches wide and three feet deep. Our job was to level off the bottom of the ditch using picks and shovels. The sun was hot and the work was tough but the pay was pretty good. After the first week of working in the ditches, we all got cleaned up and went to town to spend our hard-earned money. We ate at a restaurant and went drinking beer.

On Friday afternoon, of the second week, I was laid off. The following week, my two buddies were also let go. We had finished the job and they no longer needed us. The only money I had coming in was from playing in the band, and that wasn't much.

My uncle from Indianapolis, Indiana was coming for a visit so I decided to wait until he left to resume my search for a job. During his visit, he asked me to come home with him to spend the rest of the summer and maybe look for a job in Indianapolis. My mom agreed that I could go for a while but she really wanted me to stay around home for a little longer.

In July 1965, I left my home, my family, and all my friends and moved to Indianapolis to spend some time with my mother's younger brother. Uncle Cliff had always been one of my favorite uncles so when he and his wife extended an invitation for me to come to Indianapolis for a stay I jumped at the chance. He assured me there were plenty of jobs and I could stay as long or as short as I liked.

I packed my worldly possessions and I was off to Indianapolis to seek my fortune. A month after arriving in Indianapolis I went to work for RCA Corporation.

It was while I was working at one of the RCA warehouses that I began to hear more about Vietnam. One of the guys I worked with was going to college to avoid the draft. I didn't think much of it at the time and I hadn't formed an opinion about draft dodgers, or the war. It was still pretty much unknown to me. Occasionally I would hear something about Vietnam on the TV news but I had other things on my mind that were much more important than a war in some country that I didn't even care existed. I began running with a group of guys who were about my age and knew a little more about Vietnam than I did. All of them were very concerned about the draft and being sent off to fight in the war. Several of them got married just to avoid the draft. We soon found out that didn't work very well. I remember hearing a part of a speech by President Johnson during his visit to Indianapolis. He was talking about Vietnam and the unjust act of the Viet Cong who had just blown up a busload of Vietnamese farmers. I guess that is when I began to think more about the draft and the possibility of going to war. Because of the way I was brought up, I couldn't even think about going to college or getting married to avoid serving my country. I wasn't ready to go to college and, if I was going to get married, it would only be because I had found the woman I wanted to spend the rest of my life with.

I bought myself a brand-new Mustang, was dating a few girls and thought I was living the high life. In less than ten months all that would come to an end when I received my draft notice and was off to join the Army.

In July I got engaged, and the following day I got my draft notice. I called my parents in New Mexico to let them know the news. Dad thought I was crazy for getting married but said things would work out for me. We didn't mention the possibility of Vietnam during that phone conversation but I think we all knew I was on my way. It was as if we could make it go away by not talking about it. Out of sight, out of mind! Too bad it doesn't work that way in real life.

There were other guys I worked with who were also facing the military draft. One guy used to spend a lot of time with me talking about the draft and how he was trying to avoid it. Gary was one year older than I was and he had enrolled in college to get a deferment from the draft. To keep that deferment, he had to maintain a certain grade point average and be in good standing with the college. Although Gary was in good standing financially, his grades were bad. When he got kicked out of college he knew his days were numbered before he got his draft notice. He decided to enlist in the Air Force before he got that draft notice. If he had to go to Vietnam, the Air Force was a much safer place than the Army or Marines. Gary got his notice and joined the Air Force about thirty days before I got my draft papers. I often wondered how Gary was doing but I had no way to get in touch with him. After I got out of the service and went back to work at RCA I ran into a mutual friend. Phil told me that Gary had been killed in Vietnam shortly after he arrived at his duty station. During a mortar attack on the airstrip, Gary was running across the runway, to get to a fox hole, and received a direct hit with a mortar round. He was killed instantly.

Another guy I worked with, Ray, was a forklift operator. Ray got his notice to report to the Draft Board for a physical examination. When he reported they weighed him in and told him he was on the heavy side and that he was to lose twenty-five pounds and report back for a physical in three months. For the next three months, we never saw Ray when he wasn't eating something. He was constantly riding around on that forklift shoving candy bars in his face. He drove the forklift everywhere he went while he was at work. If you wanted to find Ray you just had to find his forklift and if he wasn't on it, he would be near-by. During that three-month period, he put on, what appeared to be, an extra fifty pounds. The cadre at the Induction Center did a lot of yelling but they couldn't force the weight off Ray. When I went into the service he was still working at the company, and still riding his forklift and eating his candy. I don't know what happened to him because he had left the company by the time I returned from the service.

Several guys I knew got married to avoid the draft, but as time went on and America's war efforts expanded in Vietnam, the marriage deferment didn't hold up for many of them. A few were successful in getting deferred then ended up divorced within the first year. They wanted to get deferred from the draft but they didn't want to get deferred from the dating scene. Although we were planning to get married I didn't want to move it up just to avoid the draft. I guess I thought I was safer than most people because my draft board was in New Mexico, and I was living in Indiana, and they would probably forget about me. I thought wrong!

CHAPTER 6

BASIC TRAINING – YOU'RE IN THE ARMY NOW!

On Friday, August 26, 1966, I reported to the Armed Forces Induction Center in Indianapolis to start my service in the US Army. I was instructed to report to the Induction Center early that morning to start processing. It was on that day that I learned the true meaning of "hurryup and wait." The Induction Center staff would walk into a room yelling at the inductees like we were deaf, and then hurriedly rush us into another room where we would stand and wait for the next portion of the processing. That process was one of the most dehumanizing experiences I have ever been through. I remember standing around in a large cold room with forty or fifty other guys, all of us naked, looking for a place to put my hands, and trying my damnedest not to look below the neck, and all the while trying to carry on a conversation that no one was interested in. We spent the day spreading our cheeks (not on our faces), pissing in bottles, and coughing on demand. After the physical checkup, the staff found work to keep us busy while we waited for the busses that would take us to Fort Knox, Kentucky. My job that day was to stuff envelopes, addressed to recent graduates from nursing schools, with letters telling them how fine the Army was and trying to get them to join up and serve their country. We all talked about how much we wanted to be there the day they processed the nurses. Finally, at the end of the day, around 5:00 P.M., the staff loaded us onto buses and we were headed south on US-31 to the United States Army Training Center, Armor, Fort Knox, Kentucky. We stopped in Columbus, Indiana for dinner at a roadside restaurant. We arrived in Fort Knox sometime after 9:00 P.M. and the nightmare really started. The drill instructors were waiting for us when the buses pulled in. They immediately started yelling at us and pulling us off the buses and shoving us into formation. These guys made the staff at the Induction Center in Indianapolis look like rank amateurs. They were hitting guys who took too long to move and shoving the rest of us around. They truly put the fear of God in us all. I was convinced at that point that the DIs (drill instructors) had the right to kill me and nobody would ask any questions.

We were all taken into a large room and given a pencil and two sheets of paper and instructed to write a letter to our mothers letting them know that we were safe and being well cared for at Fort Knox, Kentucky. The form letter we were to write was posted on a large bulletin board in front of us and we were told to copy it just like it was on the board. We addressed the envelopes and were off to pick up our bedding materials: two blankets, two sheets, one pillow, one pillow-case, and one mattress. People were struggling trying to keep everything balanced as the DIs shoved us down the line.

We were given hurried instructions that night on how to make a proper military bunk. Those who were having trouble saw their hard work ripped off the bunks and thrown across the room. Those of us who weren't having trouble managed to get by with having the bed ripped apart only once or twice. The game was to have everyone busy for the same amount of time. This was a tactic I saw used many times during my two years in the Army. I soon learned to use it to my advantage. Never be the first person to make your bed or finish cleaning your rifle. It would always be rejected on the first and second attempts to have it inspected. The key was to wait until the sergeants were getting tired of playing their games and then go for inspection. Most of the time, they would overlook a small nonconformance so they could get off duty themselves. I always took my rifle up at least twice before I submitted it late in the day for the final inspection.

During the next few days, we went through countless exercises to get equipment and uniforms before being sent to our basic training companies. Right in the middle of this exciting and fun activity, we were given a small break because of the Labor Day weekend. We got to sit around for the better part of two or three days with only minor disturbances from the DIs. Then on Monday, it started all over again. Shots, haircuts, more physical exams, and lots of tests were given during the following week and a half. Then on Wednesday, September 7th we were handed over to the staff of the Third Training Brigade, Twelfth Battalion, Company A, Fourth Platoon, and the shit really hit the fan. Our eight-week basic training was put on a short cycle of six weeks and we started to learn what it took to be a soldier in "This Man's Army."

During our waiting period, we began to give each other nicknames. It seemed like the proper thing to do since we had seen those old war movies where everyone had a nickname. If you didn't get a nickname you were destined to spend the next six weeks being called by your last name. After all, your first name was the one your mama gave you and it didn't have any place in a man's world. Besides that, our last name was printed on our uniforms and it was much easier for the DIs to read uniforms than it was to remember names. Edward Sterger was the first to get a nickname. He was wearing a shirt with what appeared to have tiger stripes on it. He ended up with the nickname of "Tiger Paws." Ed was the first guy I knew personally who *bolo*'d basic training. He thought if he failed to pass the final physical obstacle courses he would stay in basic for a long time and increase his chances of avoiding Vietnam. He was wrong. I worked with Ed after we got out of the Army. He spent a few more days on the obstacle course with a drill instructor running up his ass and soon found he could pass all the Physical Combat Proficiency Tests the Army could throw at him. He made it into Advanced Individual Training (AIT) one week after the rest of us.

I suppose because of my size I got the nickname "Sarge." The nickname stuck with me all through basic and became somewhat of a reality when I was appointed Assistant Platoon Guide. They took the two biggest guys in the platoon and made us the Platoon Guide and Assistant Platoon Guide. The Platoon Guide was a guy from Indianapolis named Ernest Martin. He was much older than the rest of us (he was in his early twenties) and I think that is what got him selected as the Platoon Guide. Ernie and I got along great and shared the responsibilities of running the platoon when the drill instructors weren't around.

In addition to being named Assistant Platoon Guide, I soon picked up the job of "Jody Man." I learned the marching cadences from the DIs and enjoyed doing them. The platoon worked out our own cadences and soon found ourselves in competition with other platoons as we marched past them. I got lots of help from one of the DIs, Staff Sergeant (SSG) Brashear. He would teach me new cadences and encourage me to put down the other platoons as they passed by. On one occasion I was called on to be the Jody Man for the whole company. It was quite an experience to try to get four platoons to sing along to the same cadence while we were marching down the road. I found myself yelling at the top of my voice trying to get the company in unison. It felt good when the whole company started singing as one large group. I later found out that SSG Brashear had a bet with some of the other platoon sergeants that I could pull it off. He got a few rounds of cold beer and I got one hell of a sore throat.

One of the squad leaders in the fourth platoon was Earl Wolfenberger from Huntington, Indiana. Earl and I became pretty good friends during the first few weeks of basic. When his girlfriend wrote him a "Dear John" letter he and I spent time talking about it. It was during those discussions that I found out he was a member of a motorcycle gang before being drafted. It just showed that once you strip people of their identity, dress them alike, and treat them like crap, they begin to find things in common with each other. Basic training was good at taking away your identity and giving you a serial number and last name only.

Before going into the Army, Edward Waggoner sold jewelry for a living. Ed was a small frail man and didn't have much physical strength. Although he had a hard time keeping up with the platoon it never stopped him from giving it his all. One such example of this came on the grenade range. Ed had a hard time throwing a hand grenade. I spent countless hours with him on the practice range trying to help with his throw. To pass this section of basic we had to throw a live hand grenade twenty-five yards with a certain amount of accuracy. Ed was only able to get the practice grenades about ten yards away from him and they never went straight. When it came time for the test with live grenades we were all concerned about Ed. One of the DIs put Ed in a parapet (concrete fox hole) with the live grenade, pulled the pin and left. He told Ed it was up to him whether he got it across the line or blew himself up. To the surprise of all of us, Ed threw that grenade well over twenty-five yards.

We also had a comedian in the platoon named Stephen Washburn. Washburn could do impersonations of several famous people. He soon picked up the ability to impersonate some of the DIs and officers. One night we were all standing around one of the bunks and Washburn went into his impersonation of Sergeant First Class (SFC) William J. McFeeley. McFeeley was our Platoon Sergeant and he lived on the first floor of our barracks in the cadre room. During Washburn's impersonation of McFeeley, he referred to him as a "Hot blooded Hawaiian taxi driver." No sooner had those words came out of Washburn's mouth when the door of the cadre room flew open and McFeeley came charging down the aisle and straight to Washburn. He grabbed Washburn around the throat with one hand and lifted him off the floor. He told Washburn if he ever heard him calling any of the platoon cadre names again he would wish he had never met him. He then put Washburn down and walked calmly back to his room. We quietly adjourned our discussions and went our separate ways. Washburn got caught doing impersonation two other times after that but neither got him in trouble. Once he was walking through the post exchange (PX) doing his impersonation of the Company Executive Officer (XO) when he turned the corner and ran into him. The lieutenant looked at Washburn, smiled and said, "Not here Washburn" and walked away. Washburn thought he was in deep shit for sure but nothing was ever said. On the second occasion, we had spent the night going through the Infiltration Course. The company commander wasn't pleased with our performance the first time so he made us go through it again. We had been called into company formation for a briefing by Captain (CPT) James H. Fowler and then left at ease while CPT Fowler took the DIs aside to talk to them. It was very dark and we couldn't see where they had gone. After about twenty minutes Washburn couldn't take the waiting any longer. He moved to the front of the company and started into his impersonation of CPT Fowler. He was on a roll when the captain walked up behind him. CPT Fowler listened to him for a while and then tapped him on the shoulder and congratulated him. We all knew Washburn was going to get in deep shit for this one but nothing was ever said except for SSG Brashear calling him a "shit bird." Washburn got called a shit bird many times during basic training.

My greatest personal triumph in basic training came when my rifle jammed on the rifle range during qualifications. Since I didn't get to shoot all my rounds I *bolo'd* that day and got punished along with the other *bolos*. As the platoon marched back to the company area that night, the *bolos* ran all the way back. We would circle the company for a while as they marched, and then one DI would stop beside the road while the company moved on. When there was about one hundred yards distance between the company and the trailing DI, we would be run back and forth between the DIs until the trailing DI caught up with the rest of the company. My insides were on fire when we reached the company area. The rest of the company was placed in formation around the sandpits while the *bolos* did the low crawl back and forth through the sand with our rifles. By this time the rifle seemed to weight about twenty pounds. If the rifle touched the sand we had to apologize to the rifle, clean it off, and go through the pit again. When we made it through the pit without getting our rifles in the sand, we had to apologize to our rifles for *boloing* on the rifle range, kiss the rifle and tell it we would never *bolo* again. While I was going through this exercise I was really pissed. I wanted to drop out from exhaustion and see what else they thought they could do to me but I wasn't going to give them the pleasure of seeing how much pain I was in. When it was all over and I got back to the barracks I dropped into my bunk and didn't move for several minutes. As I laid there I began to feel good about what I had just accomplished. I had taken the best they could throw at me and made it. For the first time in my life, I knew how far I could push my threshold of pain.

Basic training was where I first heard the expression "It doesn't rain in the Army: It rains on the Army." I still have fond memories of those long marches in the rain with my poncho neatly rolled and strapped to my web gear, wondering when we were going to be allowed to put the damn thing on. It never failed though, that after the rain stopped the DIs would halt the march and have us put on the ponchos and continue marching in the hot sun while the environment under the poncho turned into a rain forest. I never knew if this activity was planned or if the DIs were just that stupid. Either way, it didn't make much difference. Of course, we all knew by now that the DIs were in charge and they had the right to kill any of us on their slightest whim. Besides, it was good training for surviving in Vietnam during the monsoon season.

The trips through the gas chambers were among my favorite. On one occasion through the chloroacetophenone (CN) gas (a type of tear gas), we entered the room with our gas masks on and then on command we were told to take the masks off and give our name, rank, and serial number before leaving the room. This was after Washburn had called McFeeley a hot-blooded Hawaiian taxi cab driver and several of the DIs were going to make an example of Washburn. It was my luck to be in line behind Washburn when we entered the gas chamber. He removed his mask and gave the information requested but as he started to move out one of the DIs pulled him aside and told him he didn't like the way he gave his information. I pulled off my mask and gave the required information but I couldn't get out because the DI wanted to make his point really good and they were blocking the way out. I couldn't hold my breath any longer and on reflex took a deep breath of the gas. My eyes, mouth, and nose were burning like fire and, to top it off, I had my lungs full of gas now. The DI finally let Washburn go but he was so screwed-up now he couldn't find his way out. I pushed him towards the door and out of the building. As we went out he fell to the ground beside the door and I kept moving. The XO was standing just outside the door with this shit eating grin on his face looking at Washburn. As I passed by him I felt the urge to throw up. What a great chance! I leaned forward and aimed at the XO's spit-shined boots, he always had the best-looking boots in the company, and I opened my mouth and pushed with everything inside me. Just as I did the XO saw what was about to happen and realized he couldn't move in time. What came out of my mouth was the loudest belch I have ever heard and a cloud of CN gas. No liquids or other bodily fluids, just gas. What a great feeling to release all that pressure and scare the shit out of the XO all at the same time, and keep my ass out of big trouble. SSG Brashear came over to me, grabbed me, pulled me aside, and started telling me not to put any water on my face. It would react with the gas and make it burn worse. The XO was pissed but he really had no recourse against me. Washburn and I walked around for a while trying to regain our composure before the company regrouped and headed back to the company area. I soon found I couldn't call cadence and joined the ranks for the march back to the barracks.

We normally had Sunday off during basic training. We would slip into our Class A uniforms and go to the Main Post for some "real" food and a movie. We weren't allowed to have visitors until later in the training cycle. I would call Linda and talk for a while and really get homesick for her. When we were allowed to have visitors, she was uncertain about coming down by herself. Then one weekend she managed to get the nerve to make the trip on a Greyhound bus. Although it was great to see her, we only had a few precious hours and no transportation for getting out by ourselves. We took a taxi to the Main Post, had some lunch and walked around for a while. It was great to talk to someone who wasn't wearing a uniform

Tom, Fort Knox, Kentucky, 1966

and smelled good. The time passed much too quickly and before long I was putting her back on the bus for Indianapolis. As she got on the bus she said if she had known how easy it was to get to Fort Knox from Indianapolis she would have come down sooner and made more trips. There wasn't much need to cry over spilled milk now because in two more weeks I was headed to Fort Polk, Louisiana for Advanced Individual Training.

CHAPTER 7

ADVANCED INFANTRY TRAINING

I reported to Fort Polk, Louisiana on October 30th, 1966, for Advanced Individual Training (AIT). Although many of the guys from my platoon in basic training were sent to Fort Polk, I wasn't assigned with any of them that I knew. I did end up with one guy from my Basic Training Company in the same platoon with me in AIT. David Habegger was in a different platoon in basic training but we ended up in the same squad in AIT and later went to Vietnam together where we were assigned to the same battalion. In Vietnam, David worked in the Battalion Clerk's Office and I was assigned to the Ground Surveillance Section. Although we didn't spend time together daily, we kept in touch as often as possible. David was from Fort Wayne, Indiana, north of Indianapolis.

On our first day in Fort Polk's "Tigerland, Birthplace of the Combat Infantrymen for Vietnam," we were given a briefing by the battalion commander. I don't remember his name because what he had to say scared the shit out of me and I wanted to forget this man as soon as I could. He told us stories of recent events in Vietnam, complete with pictures of the dead and wounded. He also stated that he knew we were all proud to be preparing for our service in Vietnam. He said he knew we would be disappointed if we didn't get to serve there and it was his mission to make sure we were prepared and ready when the orders came down. He continued by saying he knew how much we wanted to go to Vietnam and do our part in the war and how dying for our country was an honorable thing to do. I remember thinking he was wrong about me "wanting" to go to Vietnam and therefore he was probably wrong about me getting orders to go there. All through AIT, we were betting that our company would be the exception, and get sent to Germany or Korea, or end up staying stateside to help train and process more troops. Like the song said, we were "wishing and hoping" but to no avail. The company next to ours graduated a week before we did and the whole outfit got orders for Germany. We knew without a doubt that was a sign that not all troops were being sent to Vietnam. I ran into some of those guys in Vietnam and found out they were sent to Germany for a two-week training course on armored personnel carriers (APCs), and then to Vietnam. They got to Vietnam about the same time we did.

Tiger Land was one of the strangest places I have ever been to. All along the roads, there were plywood cutouts of Viet Cong soldiers hiding behind bushes or pointing firearms at us. There were sayings every place you went, about the American soldiers' mission in Vietnam, was to make the enemy die. In December the main gate over Tiger Land was decorated with Santa, in full combat attire, sitting in a sleigh being pulled by tigers.

Company D, 4th Battalion, 3rd Training Brigade, to which I was assigned, had a mission statement posted above the orderly room door. "The mission of Delta Company is to train infantry soldiers to close and destroy the enemy by means of fire, maneuver, and close combat." Everything the DIs did during our stay was designed to meet that mission statement. We were required to always wear steel pots (helmets), and when we stepped out a door and onto the ground we were to be running when the second foot hit the ground. We were seldom allowed to walk anywhere unless we were marching in formation. We soon learned that if several of us were going to the PX, we could beat the running requirement by forming a line and marching. It was a pain in the ass but it beat the hell out of running. Every two weeks the platoon sergeants would order a company formation after dinner and march us to the barber shop to have our heads shaved. We didn't have a choice in the matter because the DIs stood by the barber chair and ordered them to shave us. David Habegger and I soon figured out that the DIs weren't watching the troops sitting on the ground outside the barbershop. We would stuff our "soft hats" inside our shirts and sit near the back of the crowd. After thirty or forty minutes we would throw our helmets into the gully behind us and slip on our soft hats and walk away. After the last guy had his head shaved and the DIs were gone we would sneak into the barber shop and get our heads shaved on the sides only, (white walls), go to the PX for a bag of Chips Ahoy! cookies and back to the barracks. The cookies were a bribe to keep the other guys from reporting us. When the DIs checked for haircuts they always did it with the helmets on so all they saw were the white walls.

We went to Leesville, Louisiana one night on pass and this old barmaid kept coming over to the table and rubbing my and David's heads and saying she couldn't trust a man with long hair. By the time we went home for Christmas leave my hair was just over a half-inch long. Not exactly a "mop head" but I had some hair for my bride to run her fingers through and I didn't look like a Monkey in my wedding pictures. Just before graduation, I got caught on a trip to the barber shop in the middle of the day. By this time several guys in the platoon were pulling the same barber shop escape tactics and the DIs were pissed. They put us in formation beside the barber shop and marched us into the shop in single file. One of the guys, with the longest hair, refused to get his hair cut. He told them they had better get the court martial papers ready because he wasn't going to allow them to cut his hair. He then broke rank and went back to the company to report what was going on to the company commander. The commanding officer (CO) sent the XO to the barber shop and stopped the head shaving, but it was too late for me. I chickened out, followed orders and got it all cut off.

In AIT I got selected as jody man again. I really had a hard time marching in close rank and did everything I could to get out of the crowd. I still had to march but if I could call cadence it kept my mind off the march. It also gave me the chance to move around a bit more. I could fall back towards the back of the platoon or move forward. I could even march backward if I wanted to and the DIs didn't get on my ass about keeping a straight line. "Dress it right and cover down," my ass! I learned more jody songs in AIT and I even started to make up a few of my own. Some of the guys in the platoon started making up jody songs and came to me to ask if I would try them out. Occasionally the DIs would call me down for trying new stuff because the platoon couldn't follow along and that sounded bad. Once or twice I got put back into the rank and file but it never lasted long. The order to march usually went something like: "Company! Platoon! Fall In; Copeland, front and center; Right face; Forward march," and I would start calling cadence. It was a great life, yea right. One of our favorite jody songs was about Dirty Lil.

> *Dirty Lil, Dirty Lil;*
> *She lives in Leesville;*
> *Never had a bath and never will;*
> *Mmmm Mmmm Dirty Lil!*

I think I met Dirty Lil the first time I went on pass to Leesville. The bars in that town were the filthiest I have ever seen. The people who worked in them seemed to fit right in with the decor, and Dirty Lil had to be one of them. I don't know if that was really her name but we gave her the title before we finished our first beer.

Our company commander was a recent graduate of West Point. He was dead set on making a record for himself, even if it killed us. Our normal day usually started at 4:00 A.M. with Physical Training (PT) and a nice long run and push-ups, lots and lots of push-ups. I must have pushed Louisiana a million miles away from my chest during AIT. Breathe wrong and you were ordered to "Drop and give me twenty," "That was too slow lady, give me twenty more." When I was in high school I was lucky to do ten push-ups in a row, and those were bad, but by the time I left Fort Polk, I could breeze through one hundred and not break a sweat. I never found myself doing any push-ups in Vietnam so I am not exactly sure what the hell that was all about.

We would have breakfast about 5:30 A.M. and load onto trucks (cattle cars) and head out for training by 6:30 A.M. If the trucks didn't show up when they were scheduled we started marching towards the training site. We were in training all day and returned to the company area around 4:30 or 5:00 P.M. Dinner was at 5:00 and by 6:00 we were back in formation and marching to an empty hangar or church or wherever the CO could find a place to hold class. We spent three or four hours reviewing everything we had learned that day. Then it was back to the barracks to clean them, our weapons, our boots, and whatever else needed cleaning before we hit the sack between 1:00 and 1:30 A.M. Two or three hours of uninterrupted sleep and we started over again. Our company set new post training records on every course. It was this type of training that probably kept me alive in Vietnam. You didn't have to think about what to do in an emergency, it had been drilled in and came as second nature when you needed it.

Some mornings, while waiting on the trucks to arrive, we would sit around outside the barracks. We were not allowed to go back in and get comfortable no matter what the weather. The barracks at Fort Polk were built on concrete pillars that were about twenty-four inches tall and eighteen inches in diameter. Someone discovered that they could crawl under the barracks and lay behind those posts and get some shuteye without getting caught. We all started taking turns standing watch while our buddies got a few extra minutes of sleep. As time went by, there were more people under the barracks and fewer people keeping watch, but the DIs never seemed to catch on. We were also given ten-minute smoke breaks during training classes. Those of us who didn't smoke started laying on the ground or leaning against buildings and taking short naps. This really pissed the DIs off but the CO stepped in and said we could do whatever we wanted with our breaks if we were not late falling in after the break. Again, the buddy system kicked in and we took care to see that no one was late for fall in. I remember looking around one day, during a rain shower, and noticing that no more than half a dozen people were in the upright position. It looked as if a mortar round had landed in the middle of a formation and killed the whole group. Poncho covered bodies were lying everywhere. Once fall in was called it only took seconds for everyone to be on their feet.

When we were lucky enough to get a ride on trucks to training we were put into "cattle cars." There were bench seats down both sides of the trailer and a double bench seat down the middle. We would get in the cattle cars and sit as close as possible, we thought. The DIs would always manage to get a few more men on the trailer by hanging from the top frame and swinging in and kicking the ones on the end to push them down a couple of seats. By the time the trailers were loaded to suit the DIs, it became another great place to catch a nap. We were packed in so tight you couldn't fall left, right, forward, or backward. I guess it was kind of like being back in the womb, only with full combat gear. The rides to the training areas were thirty to forty minutes long. Most days I could manage to nap for the major part of the ride. On occasion, I would look around the trailer and notice that most of the men were asleep. Once we got to the training area the hurryup and wait crap started again. As we were getting off the trailers the DIs would grab our web gear and pull us off. It is a tossup whether this activity slowed down or sped up the unloading process. The first few guys got pulled off sideways and they would fall to the ground on top of each other. The unloading had to stop while they gathered their equipment and scrambled out of the way. Once you had room to face the door you could usually make a low running jump off the trailer and get clear of the ones behind you. The whole time, the DIs were standing there pulling and pushing and yelling "Move out ladies. We have a war waiting for your sorry asses."

Once we were unloaded we were quickly called into formation and started running from place to place. It wasn't unusual for us to run to the training area and then wait for the class ahead of us to finish before we could move in. While waiting we were kept busy with useless drills and constant harassment. I spent thirty minutes one day wiping the smile off my face, throwing it on the ground and stomping on it. Several times after stomping the smile into the ground I was ordered to put dirt over it and give it a righteous burial. The DI was really getting pissed at me but it was about the stupidest exercise I had ever been forced to do. I couldn't stop smiling and laughing. The more I seemed to find humor in this exercise, the more it pissed off the DI. I am surprised he didn't have me chamber a round into my M14 and shoot the damn smile. All in all, the exercise kept us in formation and busy until the instructor was ready for us in class.

When we went to map reading class it was pouring down rain. We spent most of the morning inside a large hangar reading maps and doing exercises. At the break, we were forced to go outside and stand in the rain, "so we could get some fresh air." After lunch, the rain let up and we went outside to practice our overland navigation skills. We were given a map and compass and told to travel given distances in given directions and were to meet at a location three or four miles away. We traveled in groups and used the landscape for reference points. It was an easy exercise but there was one group of guys from Detroit, Michigan who had never been out of the city and had a tough time negotiating the course. Around 5:00 P.M. we were served dinner and went back into the classroom for more instruction until night fell. When it was dark we were taken back to the navigation course and sent off in another direction. This time we had to take compass readings off the stars or whatever we could make out in the dark. It was a lot tougher at night but most groups made it through fine. About an hour into the exercise we heard the guys from Detroit yelling and laughing. They ran into a heard of cows and thought they were being charged. They scattered in several different directions and then had to regroup. When they found each other, they were off course and lost. It was well after midnight before they made it to the rendezvous point, and that was because the DIs went out and found them and brought them in.

I developed a friendship with one of those guys from Detroit. His name was Bobby Lewis but about three weeks into AIT I gave him the nickname of "Teddy Bear." Bobby had the bunk next to mine and every night when we finished our training and were cleaning the barracks, Bobby would get in his bunk and go to sleep. If we stayed on his ass he would get up and do his share but he tried to get by with doing as little as possible. I got tired of him going to sleep so I would wake him up and ask him where his Teddy Bear was. He would wake up, look at me and repeat the words "Where is my Teddy Bear." He would then roll over and say, "Leave me alone mother fucker," and go back to sleep. I would wait until he went to sleep and do it again. When he went home on Christmas leave he woke up almost every night asking his wife where his Teddy Bear was. After that, the nickname stuck. When we got to Vietnam and he got to be an APC Commander he painted Teddy Bear on the side of the APC and flew his wife's bra from the radio aerial.

There were two sayings that the DIs used that we got really tired of. "You ain't goin' home" and "Sorry 'bout that." We all knew that we were supposed to get a two week leave for Christmas but every time we screwed-up the DIs would start yelling, "you ain't goin' home." Or if we screwed up in training they would say, "You going to Vietnam, and you are going to screw up like this, and Charlie is going to kill your sorry ass, and you ain't never goin' home, well sorry 'bout that." On occasion, the DIs would catch one of the guys in a down mood because they got a "Dear John" letter or some other bad news from home and they would start hammering on them with, "So, 'Jody' got your girl, did he? Well sorry 'bout that." Or, "you are going to go to Vietnam, and Charlie is going to zap your ass, and your mother is going to get a letter from the Army saying 'Sorry 'bout that.'" I guess this was supposed to build character but most of us didn't get it.

We finally made it to Christmas leave and the DIs pulled their ridiculous shit again. We were dressed in our class A uniforms, and they decided to march us to the bus depot via a muddy field instead of down the streets. By the time we got there, our "spit-shined" shoes (that we didn't get to wear but three times at Fort Polk) were covered with mud and the mud was smeared up our pant legs. We were going to get a rash of shit from every military policeman (MP) we ran into at every bus terminal or airport until we got home.

David Habegger's wife had arranged to reserve airline tickets for us from Shreveport, Louisiana back to Indiana. Other people were trying to fly out of Leesville but the flights were booked solid for days. We took a bus from Fort Polk to Shreveport and a man, whom Dave's wife did business with in Shreveport, picked us up at the bus terminal and took us to his business. We cleaned off the mud the best we could and he took us out for lunch and on to the airport. I got back to Indianapolis around 10:00 P.M. on Friday night and went to my uncle's house. When I got there, I noticed the lights were still on at my girlfriend's house. We were getting married on Sunday and I couldn't wait to see her. I left my bags on my uncle's porch and went to Linda's house hoping that she would be up. She had just gone to bed but her mother went up and got her. It was great to see her and we talked for a couple of hours. I pinned one of my shooting marksmanship badges on her housecoat and said good night. When I got back to my uncle's house, he was a little pissed that I had put my bags on the porch and left, but, he didn't give me much grief over it. We talked for several hours and went to bed.

On Saturday, Linda and I took all my dirty clothes to the laundromat and laundered them. All my underwear was yellowed from the laundry service at Fort Polk so she bleached the hell out of them. Several weeks later they fell apart from all the bleach and I had to buy all new boxer shorts. She also took the time to iron the fly so it would stay shut on every pair of boxers I had. They were very white and wrinkle-free right up to the day they fell apart.

On Sunday we got married in a small ceremony with only my uncle and aunt there to witness it. Following the wedding, we went back to Linda's house for a small reception, with fewer than a dozen people, and we were off on our honeymoon. We drove all the way to Speedway, Indiana, about fifteen miles, and stayed in the Holiday Inn for a couple of days. We had very little money so we couldn't go far or stay long. We spent the rest of my Christmas leave moving between her parents' home and my uncle's home. During the week we would stay at my uncle's home because they both worked and we could be alone. We spent weekends with her family, including Christmas. Then we went back to my uncle's house for New Year's Eve.

All during our time together we tried not to talk about Vietnam. One night we were having a late snack and one of those Hallmark Theater presentations came on. The title was *Ollie's Last War*. It was about a black man named Ollie who went to Vietnam and managed to get separated from his outfit. He hated the Vietnamese people but found himself depending on them to hide him from the enemy. While he was hiding he fell in love with a Vietnamese woman and began to lose his hatred for the Vietnamese. The movie ended with him getting killed. That was more than Linda could stand and she really let the emotions go. We spent the rest of the night talking about Vietnam and holding each other very close. I tried my damnedest to convince her that I wasn't going to get killed and that I would see her in a few months. I don't think I ever convinced her, but we agreed not to talk about it anymore. I didn't do a good job of convincing myself either, but I was trying to make the best out of the time we had to together before I went back to Fort Polk to finish my training.

After two weeks at home with Linda, we packed my bags and I was off to Fort Polk for another two weeks of training.

Linda and I didn't have much money (I think I was getting paid $92 per month) so I bought a bus ticket back to Louisiana. After a tearful good-bye at the bus terminal in Indianapolis, I was on my way. The first stop was Saint Louis, Missouri for a four-hour layover and a change of buses. I called Linda from the bus terminal, thinking that would lift my spirits, but it only made it worse. The time passed and I got on the bus headed south. As I sat on the bus waiting for it to finish loading I looked out the window in a half daze. I could see the reflection of myself in the glass as people were passing by, most of whom were servicemen trying to get back to their duty stations. Suddenly, I noticed that I was picking up my duffle bag and turning to walk away. I came out of the daze and watched at what I had previously thought was my reflection walk to the next bus and get on. I had always heard that we all have an exact double somewhere in the world and I had just seen mine. It was the eeriest thing I had ever experienced. I heard the bus door close, the engine start, and we were on the way. The bus traveled all night and I managed to sleep most of the way. I was awakened by the driver somewhere in the "Deep South" and told the bus was at the end of its run. To this day I do not know where I was but I waited there for an hour or so until the bus to Fort Polk pulled in. When I loaded on the bus I sat next to a guy from Indianapolis. I hadn't noticed him on the other buses but he had been there. We got to talking about Indianapolis and discovered that we both had worked at RCA before being drafted and knew several of the same people. His name is Sonny Overstreet and I ran into him often at RCA after we got out of the service. Sonny was assigned to another training company at Fort Polk but he had started his training cycle the same time I did. We had lunch together a couple of times on weekends at Fort Polk, but, never really spent much time together.

When I got back to my training company, the next few weeks consisted mostly of field exercises. One week was spent on bivouac on Peason Ridge, a simulated Vietnam training area. There were exercises every night and constant harassment by the drill instructors. It was cold and rainy and we all wanted to be somewhere else. I did manage to get my mind off Linda and back onto becoming a lean, mean, fighting machine. The cooks served up hot vegetable soup around midnight almost every night. That soup was the only thing that made it bearable.

There was a six-hole latrine setup in the center of the Night Defensive Perimeter (NDP). It was a large box with three toilet seats on each side. One of the DIs was taking a dump when two of the soldiers he had just harassed came up behind the latrine. When they recognized who was sitting on the latrine they decided it was time for a little payback. One of the guys lifted the seat behind the DI and the other stuck his M14 into the hole and positioned the muzzle directly under the DI's ass. He fired off a couple of blank rounds and they took off. The muzzle flash from the M14 managed to put some minor burns on the DI's ass and he was sent to the medics, who sent him back to the company area for the rest of the exercise. He never saw who shot him but he tried to find out until the day we left for Vietnam.

One night the perimeter was attacked by wild pigs. These were domestic pigs that had wandered away from farms years ago and were living and breeding in the wilds of Fort Polk. The guys from two or three foxholes started firing blanks at the pigs and when they turned to run away they chased them through the woods. One guy fixed his bayonet and as the pigs ran into the woods he threw his rifle like a spear in the direction of the pigs. He missed the pig but managed to bury his bayonet into a tree. He wiggled the rifle around trying to get the bayonet out of the tree but all he managed to do was break off the blade. When we left Fort Polk, he turned in the bayonet handle with less than one inch of blade in the sheath.

While we were on bivouac, we performed a house-to-house search in a Vietnamese village. Everything in the village was booby-trapped with small explosive simulators. Step on a ramp and it would blow up; open a door and it would blow up. Every damn way you turned something was exploding in your face. The DIs were pushing us to enter houses and open gates without taking our time to look them over properly. David Habegger, Jim Childs, Russ Sign, and I broke away from the main body and started doing our own house-to-house search. We started looking for the explosives and taking them down before they blew up. The Platoon Guide, Casey, joined in with us and we took down about a half dozen simulators. When we joined the rest of the platoon we were told to open doors that were supposed to explode, but we had already disarmed them. It took all the fun out of it for the DIs.

During our last week at Fort Polk, we were on the machine gun range. We spent most of the day learning how to clean and fire M60 .50 caliber machine guns. At the end of the day, most of us were finished and were standing around waiting for the rest of the company. The company commander had driven his MG sports car out to the range that day and it was parked near where we were assembled. Casey slipped over to the car and attached one of the booby trap simulators to the drive shaft of the MG. When the "Old Man" started backing his car up there was one hell of an explosion. The parking lot was covered with a cloud of dust and the explosion raised enough dust to make the MG disappear. The "Old Man" got out of the car really pissed. He had the DIs call the company to assembly and as he walked back and forth in front of the company waiting for everyone to fall in you could see the anger on his face. Once we were all in formation he walked back and forth for several minutes and then turned to address the company. He suddenly got a smile on his face and said, "It is apparent to me from your performance during this training cycle that you are the best soldiers ever produced at Fort Polk. You have studied hard and learned your lessons well. The explosion under my car has proven to me without a doubt that you men are ready to take your place in Vietnam. I do not know who planted the booby trap and I do not want to know. I salute you all for a job well done." Having said that, he pulled himself to attention and gave us his best West Point salute, walked to his car, and drove away.

The next day we were told to pack our belongings and prepare for graduation and departure. While we were packing, the DI with the burnt ass called us all to assembly and marched us down to the barber shop to have our heads shaved. The following day we went through our graduation ceremony and I headed back to Indiana for a final week with my wife, and then to New Mexico for a week with my parents, before flying to California and on to Vietnam.

Although I developed friendships with several people during AIT only one of them withstood the test of time. Jim Childs is from Kawkawlin, Michigan. We became close friends in AIT but our friendship became even closer after we were out of AIT and in Vietnam. There were four of us who stayed close during training; David Habegger, Jim Childs, Russ Sign, and me. We stuck together during all the field exercises and helped each other get through the tough times. During the survival, escape, and evasion exercise we were a team. We were given some rice, a can of green beans, a can of pineapple, a chicken, and an empty gallon can. We built our fire and cooked our meal. Jim had the same outdoor experiences as a kid that I did. Russ and Dave built the fire and Jim and I cooked the meal. We roasted the chicken over the open fire and only dropped it in the fire once or twice. It wasn't the best chicken I ever ate but once we scraped the ash off, it was edible. We warmed up the green beans in the can and passed it around and each of us ate out of the can. We boiled some water in the gallon can and fixed the rice. We couldn't figure out what to do with the pineapple so we dumped it in with the rice. The pineapple juice sweetened the rice and it tasted pretty good mixed together.

Following dinner, we were moved into bleachers for an orientation. We knew what to expect from talking to other soldiers who had been through the exercise. We sat at the top of the bleachers and could look east, down the road toward the dump that Jim and I had been to just a few days earlier. We had a good understanding of where we were and how to make our escape when the invaders captured us. When the shit hit the fan, we went over the back of the bleachers and headed east down the road towards the dump. After about a hundred meters or so we got off the road and into the cover of the bushes. We moved parallel to the road until we reached the intersecting road that ran into the dump. We then headed north towards the area we were told the trucks would be waiting to take us back to the barracks. Russ boasted about his ability to navigate through the woods in the dark and took the lead. He was doing such a great job of finding every water-filled sinkhole along the way that within the first hour he was soaked from the waist down. We decided to move back onto the road to make better time. We stayed close to the edge so we could duck quickly back into the woods if the need arose. And it did on several occasions. The road was busy with trucks and Jeeps taking prisoners to the POW camp. We managed to make our way back into the woods in enough time to avoid detection. When we got close to the POW camp we could hear the captors yelling at the prisoners. We crawled through the woods to get a better look. We could see the bright lights and hear guys yelling as they were pushed and shoved against walls and into tanks of stagnant water. The cadre was making the experience seem as real as possible. We backtracked through the woods to the road and headed north. When we got to the pickup area we were the first to arrive. I suggested we stay inside the tree line and watch for a while. It took about fifteen minutes before the first troops walked into the pickup area. About six to eight guys walked in and started to make themselves comfortable. We heard the cadre start yelling at them and watched as they took their weapons away from them, tied their hands behind their backs and loaded them into the trucks. One of the DIs was heard to say that they must have cheated because nobody could make it through the course in that short of a time. We moved back into the woods and stayed very low for a long time. Only after we saw lots of guys standing around did we decide to venture into the pickup area. We stood around the trucks freezing our asses off for about an hour. Then we were loaded into the trucks and taken to a large warehouse for the debriefing. It was the decision of the cadre that the company had failed the exercise. During the interrogations at the camp, they obtained a complete roster of names for the company. Several guys broke during the interrogation and gave information, including the home addresses of their wives and girlfriends. The company that had done so well all through AIT, had set new post records in almost everything we did, had now really screwed up on the final exercise. What the hell were they going to do to us, "Send us to Vietnam"?

During those late nights cleaning the barracks, Jim Childs taught us all to do the "Stockade Shuffle." We spent many nights in the barracks, following a long day of training, listening to music, and doing the Stockade Shuffle. We made quite a picture, half a dozen guys dressed in their long johns and soft caps, moving through the barracks in a single file line, doing the Stockade Shuffle. To this day I don't know if Jim made up the Stockade Shuffle or if someone had shown it to him. It is amazing what grown men will stoop to in order to entertain themselves. The Shuffle went something like this:

Start by standing at attention.

Bend slightly forward at the waist while raising your left foot and moving it forward about eighteen inches.

Place your left foot on the floor and while slowly dragging your right foot forward, bend your arms at the elbows and bring your hands parallel with the floor and snap your fingers.

At this point, you are back at attention and ready to repeat the movement all over again.

One guy on the second floor of the barracks had a portable record player and he would play songs and join in the Shuffle line. The guys from Detroit would sit at the end of the barracks playing cards and refer to us as "crazy white mother fuckers."

As I said earlier, I went home during Christmas leave and got married. Jim Childs had been talking about getting married but Sharon's parents were against it. Sharon's mom and dad got married just before he went off to fight in World War II. Sharon's dad served in Burma as a Ranger and had some tough times when he came home. Jim and I talked a lot about whether it made sense to get married before going to Vietnam and I told him I didn't see that it made that much difference. Linda and Sharon would be just as devastated if we stayed single and got killed as they would if we were married. At least if we were married they would get that $10,000 GI insurance policy to help them get over it. Jim laughed and went to call Sharon. During our two-week leave between AIT and shipping off to Vietnam, Jim and Sharon got married with the blessings of both families.

When we got to Vietnam Jim and I went to separate units. I remembered his home address and after a couple of months, I wrote to his wife and asked for his military address. For the first few months, we communicated more through Sharon than we did through the US Army's in-country mail system. After leaving Vietnam, Jim and I were both stationed at Fort Hood, Texas. I was in the First Armored Division and Jim was in the Second Armored Division. We spent five months at Fort Hood with our wives before getting out of the Army. During this time, we developed a lasting friendship.

CHAPTER 8

OAKLAND BOUND, OR CALIFORNIA HERE I COME

After graduation from AIT I got a two week leave before I had to report to Oakland, California for processing to Vietnam. I flew to Indianapolis, Indiana to spend a week with my wife and then to Hobbs, New Mexico to spend a week with my parents. My Uncle Charles and Brother-in-law Gene drove me to El Paso, Texas to catch a flight to California.

I flew from El Paso, Texas to Phoenix, Arizona on Continental Airlines. The combination of lack of sleep and the beers I drank with my brother-in-law and uncle kicked in big time shortly after leaving the ground in El Paso, so there wasn't much to remember about the flight. I do remember watching the stewardess walking up the aisle and thinking of the commercial Continental was running; "We really move our tails for you." Of course, they always showed the golden tail of an airplane, but we all knew which tails they were really talking about. The stop in Phoenix was a short one and didn't require a plane change before we continued to Los Angeles. We landed at LAX around 4:00 A.M. and I had several hours to kill before the flight to San Francisco departed. I walked around the airport for a while and looked at what few things there are to look at before an airport wakes up. Around 6:00 A.M. I decided to call my brother, who was living in Long Beach and let him know I was on my way to Vietnam. I thought he might drive to the airport and spend some time with me, but I had waited too long to call him, and there wasn't time for him and his family to make it to the airport before I had to leave. We talked for a while and he promised me he would write to me often. Having been in the Navy for six years he knew how lonely I was going to be and how much a letter from home would mean. I got one short note in a Christmas card from him during my tour of duty. I guess the Navy didn't get as homesick as the Army.

I stopped in the Host Coffee Shop and had some breakfast and a piece of cheesecake before reporting to the gate to catch the plane to San Francisco. When I got to San Francisco there were signs in the terminal directing all military personnel who were reporting to the Oakland Army Terminal to go to a certain location in the airport. I found my way through the crowd and was greeted by an Army Staff Sergeant who directed me onto a bus. I don't remember much about the ride from the airport to the Army Terminal, or much about the Army Terminal itself. I do remember the never-ending sea of young men, all dressed in green or khaki, and all headed for the same place I was going. I had been promoted to Private First Class (PFC) before leaving Fort Polk but hadn't bothered to get the stripes sewn onto my uniforms before I left. I didn't see much use in spending the money to have stripes sewn on since they were going to take away the standard issue uniforms in Vietnam and give me jungle fatigues. I soon found a reason to get those stripes on. All the slick sleeves were being assigned to make-work details just to keep them busy. Anyone who had the rank of PFC and above was being given special privileges, one of the very few I ever got in the Army. I dug out my orders to prove I was a PFC and quickly found a place to get some stripes sewn on. I then reported to the Processing Center and officially started my journey to Vietnam.

After evening mess, I went to an enlisted men's club and had a few beers and some munchies. I didn't feel much like partying so I went back to my bunk to write letters to my wife and my mom. The bunk was in the middle of a large hanger with what seemed like thousands of other guys. There were rows and rows of bunks stacked two high. I settled in and wrote a few letters to my loved ones. It made me feel closer to the ones I wasn't going to see for twelve months so I felt better when I dropped the letters in the mail. After a quick trip to the mailbox, I returned to my bunk and dropped off to sleep around 9:00 P.M. I suddenly awoke at 1:00 A.M. looking for a place to throw up. I found a butt can sitting nearby and filled it to the rim. The guy in the top bunk woke up and asked if I was OK. "Too much beer will do that every time," he said. It wasn't the beer, it was the realization of where I was about to go in a few hours and the fear that I would never see the ones I loved again. It was at that time I decided if I was going to survive in Vietnam I had to keep a positive attitude and never think about dying again. With that thought in mind, I drifted back into a fitful sleep.

The next morning, we fell out for breakfast and several more hours of processing paperwork and getting travel orders. With my newly attached stripes, one on each sleeve, and my ability to look extremely busy I could avoid most of the work details. My luck and bullshit didn't hold out and I was given a broom and told to sweep a large area of concrete that I thought looked perfectly clean. When the NCO (non-commissioned officer) walked away I leaned the broom against the building and got the hell out of there. What were they going to do, send me to Vietnam? I skipped lunch and just walked around the fence of the Oakland Terminal looking through the wire at the last vestige of safety and freedom I would see for a while. In the Oakland Bay, just west of the Terminal, I watched as a ship slowly sailed by. I began to realize that the world was going on with its day-to-day activities and wasn't paying much attention to what was happening in Vietnam. How the hell could all those people be so unconcerned about America's best and bravest being shipped off to fight in a war that most of us knew very little about? Damn Communism anyway!

Late in the afternoon, I was loaded onto a bus for the airport and the final American leg of my journey to Vietnam was about to begin. While we were waiting at the airport gate for the airplane to be prepared, the Governor of California, Ronald Reagan, walked through the terminal area. He quickly came over and started shaking our hands and telling us how nice it was to have us home from Vietnam. As he walked away he turned, waved, and shouted, "Welcome Home Boys." I felt as though I were trapped in a cross between *The Twilight Zone* and *Death Valley Days*. At least he had the decency to come over and acknowledge our existence even though he didn't know if we were coming or going. That small deed got him my vote when he ran for president.

We loaded the plane and were off to Hawaii. The plane was from Braniff Airlines with the colorful paint job. This was the first time I had ever flown over a large body of water. I can remember looking down and searching the vast expanse of water below for islands and boats with the idea that I would know which way to swim if the plane went down. The flight was uneventful until we reached Hawaii. When the pilot lowered the landing gear a hydraulic line burst and sprayed hydraulic fluid through the seams in the wall and into the cabin. We were grounded in Hawaii while the ground crew fixed the problem. I remember walking through the terminal area of the airport and thinking about going AWOL (absent without leave). The air was filled with the smell of tropical flowers and it felt great. I never wanted to leave. I would call my wife and have her fly over and we would just stay there for the rest of our lives. Instead, I went to the Host snack bar and ordered a piece of that great cheesecake and a Coke. As I sat there enjoying my snack I kept thinking about how nice it would be to just stay there, but I had a duty to serve my country and that should come first. After a three-hour delay, an announcement came over the PA system to report back to the plane and we were once again airborne.

When the plane touched down in Manila we experienced problems again. One of the tires blew out and once again we found ourselves grounded, waiting for hours while they flew in a replacement tire. It was the middle of the night and everything in the terminal building was closed. We were ordered to stick close to the terminal and not wander off. Some of the old timers jumped into a taxi and headed for a nearby bar. Having been there before, they knew where to go for a cold beer. The rest of us stayed around wherever we could find a place to sit or lay and waited. It was well after midnight before we were back on the plane and headed for Vietnam.

The guy sitting next to me was returning to Vietnam from the States after being sent home on emergency leave. All during the flight, he hadn't said much to any of us. He talked a little about his emergency leave and how he was pulled out of the jungle and put on a plane back to the States without a shower or a change of uniform. He said he didn't know how bad he looked and smelled until he was seated in the airplane. Then it was too late to do much about it. Most of the time during our flight, he just sat there and stared ahead into a place the rest of us knew nothing about. A place we didn't understand, but would learn about over the next few months, and would live with for the rest of our lives. His silence was suddenly broken when he looked out the window of the plane and quietly said, "We are here. I can smell the rice paddies and the buffalo shit." I leaned forward and looked out the window for my first glimpse of Vietnam. I expected to see battles raging across the countryside but instead I was greeted with total darkness below. The only things I saw outside the airplane were the marker lights on the wing tips. A few minutes later the pilot announced that we were over the coast of Vietnam and would be landing in Saigon in fifteen minutes. As we came in over the country I once again looked out the window, but this time, I could see a few fires off in the distance. I wondered what was going on and what we would be getting into when we landed. One of the DIs at Fort Polk had told us there were foxholes every few feet between the airplane and the terminal building. If we got sniper fire, and we most likely would, we were to move from hole to hole until we got into the terminal building. I didn't believe him when he was telling us that story at Fort Polk, but now that we were in Vietnam, those thoughts began racing through my mind and I could feel my heart pounding deep inside my chest.

Shortly after the plane landed the pilot turned off all the lights and we taxied across the airport in a darkened airplane. Everyone was trying to look out the windows but there just weren't enough windows to go around. Some military vehicles pulled alongside and escorted us to the terminal. "What the hell is going on and why the hell am I here?"

As we got off the plane the stewardesses were lined up at the bottom of the steps. One of the stewardesses was sobbing openly. As we passed by, she was kissing and hugging as many GIs as she could. I wondered how many soldiers she had kissed who had never gotten their return ticket on the Freedom Bird. As I got my hug I told her I would see her in twelve months and then quickly looked around for those foxholes.

CHAPTER 9

GREEN MEETS GREEN, MY ARRIVAL IN VIETNAM

I arrived in Vietnam on February 3, 1967, and walked across the runway in the predawn darkness and into the terminal building. No foxholes, no snipers, no dodging and weaving for cover, but there were MPs positioned every few yards along the way. We were quickly processed into Vietnam and put onto buses for the trip to the Long Binh Replacement Processing Center outside of Saigon. As I settled into my seat on the bus I noticed the windows were covered with heavy metal screens. The screens would stop hand grenades from being thrown into the bus but I didn't think they would do much to stop a bullet. I began to get a little uneasy about this situation. When the bus was loaded, the MPs mounted their Jeeps and I watched as one of them loaded a round into the chamber of his M60 machine gun. Now I was getting really uneasy. There were thirty to forty of us on the bus with no weapons and we were being escorted by six MPs with light weapons.

As we drove through the streets, in darkness, I strained my eyes looking for anything that might be an ambush. I had no concept of where I was or my location relative to the war. All I knew was that I was in Vietnam and a war was going on. During my training at Fort Polk, we were taught that Viet Cong soldiers wore black pajamas. As I looked around I was starting to see people in black pajamas. Now I was scared shitless.

We arrived at the Replacement Center and were rushed into a Quonset hut with lines of tables running along both sides. One side was for processing into Vietnam and the other side was for processing out of Vietnam. As we were processing in, the other side of the building started to fill up with men who were leaving. They all were very tan and thin and moved quietly through the line. A few of them began ribbing us about how thankful they were that we had come to replace them. They called us "FNGs, (Fucking New Guys)," "Cherries," and "Greenies." It would be a year before I could return the favor, and I did just that.

We were taken to a tent and given a place to sleep. I didn't bother to undo the "S" roll of my mattress, I just leaned against it and looked out the side of the tent into the darkness. I didn't know what was out there and I sure as hell wasn't going to close my eyes and let some slant-eyed son of a bitch slip in and cut my throat. It was several days before I got any meaningful sleep in Vietnam.

When daylight came I could see more American military installations surrounding the Replacement Center and I started to feel a little more secure, but I still didn't have a gun. Later, I would look back on my first few days in Vietnam and laugh at how scared I was and how secure I felt in those same surroundings after a few months in country. In time, I developed the ability to fall asleep in all sorts of situations, and could even sleep through the downpour of the monsoon rain. I also developed the ability to wake from a deep sleep just seconds before someone touched me or spoke my name, to wake me for my turn on guard duty. I could fall into a deep sleep within seconds and awaken from it even quicker with all my senses intact. It was years after leaving the service before I could sleep all through the night, without waking every couple of hours to look out the window, or just stare around the room into the darkness.

The celebration of the Tet New Year of 1967 was just starting to get underway in Vietnam. On the third night at the center, I was placed on guard duty and given a rifle with one magazine of ammunition. I was instructed not to put the magazine into the rifle unless given a direct order to do so. Bullshit! When I got to my position, I placed the magazine into the rifle but didn't latch it in. If the guard commander came by, I could quickly slip it out, but I wasn't about to leave it out. I was placed in a sandbagged guard post by myself with an M14 rifle, twenty rounds of ammo, and a field telephone. The telephone connected me with the other guard posts and eventually with the guard commander. All night long we were kept busy ringing each other and doing communication checks. Then, shortly after midnight, the war came to life for the FNGs. The guy in the guard post next to the gate had suddenly opened fire and the adrenaline was flowing like mad in all of us. I hadn't been this excited about firing a rifle since I saw my first deer. I quickly latched the magazine into the rifle and put a round into the chamber. I was scared as hell and ready for a fight. I was dangerous! The field phone started ringing and I picked up the handset. The guard commander was trying to find out what was going on and we were tasked with relaying the message from post-to-post via the telephone. We eventually found out that some kids had run past the guard post and thrown a bunch of firecrackers at the guard. The explosion of the firecrackers startled the guard and he returned fire. He had emptied all twenty rounds into the surrounding neighborhood but had missed everyone. We were instructed to tell him to remove the magazine from his rifle, place the rifle across the bunker from him, and sit on the floor until they could get someone up there to relieve him. We all settled down and about 3:00 A.M. it started again. Off to my left the perimeter lit up and one of the guards fired a few rounds into the jungle in front of him. A monkey had set off a trip flare and quickly left the area. I didn't sleep at all that night. When daylight came we could see that we were located next to another military installation with only twenty to thirty meters of brush between us. A day or so later, one of the FNGs on guard duty put a round in his shotgun, placed it to his foot and pulled the trigger. The cadre called us all together to tell us about this "chickenshit act of cowardice" and to let us know that the man would be charged with self-inflicting bodily injury to avoid military duty and eventually sent to prison. Just in case the rest of us saw that alternative as an easy way out.

During the day we continued our processing and waiting for unit assignments. It was in the Replacement Center that I got my first experience at burning shit. Six of us were randomly selected to clean the inside of the latrines. As we finished our work and started to leave, an old staff sergeant placed us on the shit-burning detail. It appeared the guys selected for that job had taken off while the sergeant was having a drink at the NCO club. He came back to find several half barrels of shit sitting outside the latrines and no one to burn them. Although we argued that we had done our share, it was no use. He had lost one crew and he wasn't about to lose another. We poured diesel fuel into the barrels of shit and set them on fire. They burned for a while but the shit was still there. We began to throw more diesel fuel on the burning barrels and before long we had one hell of a fire going. A huge column of black smoke rose high into the air. It looked as though an airplane had crashed and was burning. The smell was the worst thing I had ever experienced.

The smoke and flames began to attract a lot of attention. As I stood there wondering what we were going to do if there was still shit in the barrels when the fire went out I heard a familiar voice. I turned around and standing next to me was SFC McFeeley, my basic training Platoon Sergeant. He had spotted me because of the rather large fire and came over to buy me a beer. I pointed out the SSGT in charge of the operation and he quickly pulled rank and we were off to the (Enlisted Men's) EM Club. I never thought I would be glad to see McFeeley, but this was a much different person than I had known in basic training. We were both assigned to the

First Infantry Division and stationed in Lai Khe but in different battalions. I saw him several more times during my tour in Vietnam and began to know him as a true leader who showed a lot of concern for his men.

During the rest of my time in the "repo depot" I managed to avoid any more details by figuring out the schedule used to assign details and avoiding those times and places.

I was introduced to reconstituted milk and milk products while in the Replacement Center. One morning as I was going through the chow line I noticed that no one was taking any milk. I asked the cook if it was OK to take the milk and he told me to take all I wanted. I filled my canteen cup as full as I could and found a table. I dug into the chow and had a mouth full when I decided to wash it down with a big swallow of ice cold milk. I got a mouth full of milk and had started to swallow before I noticed the rotten taste. I was trapped in the center of a table and I couldn't get out fast enough to get rid of the milk so I swallowed it. The gag reflexes immediately took over and it took everything I had to keep from throwing up. The guys around me started laughing and asking me how long I had been in country (like any of us had been there more than a week). It would be months before I tried milk again.

I had my first experience with the Vietnamese language at the Replacement Center. As we sat having lunch one day some Vietnamese girls walked by the tent. One of the guys stationed at the Replacement Center told us that if we wanted to call a Vietnamese over we should say "lai day." I decided to try it out. I looked at the girls and with confidence shouted out "lai day, lai day." The girls stopped and walked over to the tent. One of them came forward and asked me what I wanted. I had no idea what to say at that point so I just looked at her. She stood there for a minute and then mumbled "You fuck you muther you" and walked away. So much for my first Vietnamese lesson.

On about the fifth day in country I was assigned to the First Infantry Division, the Big Red One. I didn't know much about them but I soon learned that "If you are going to be one,

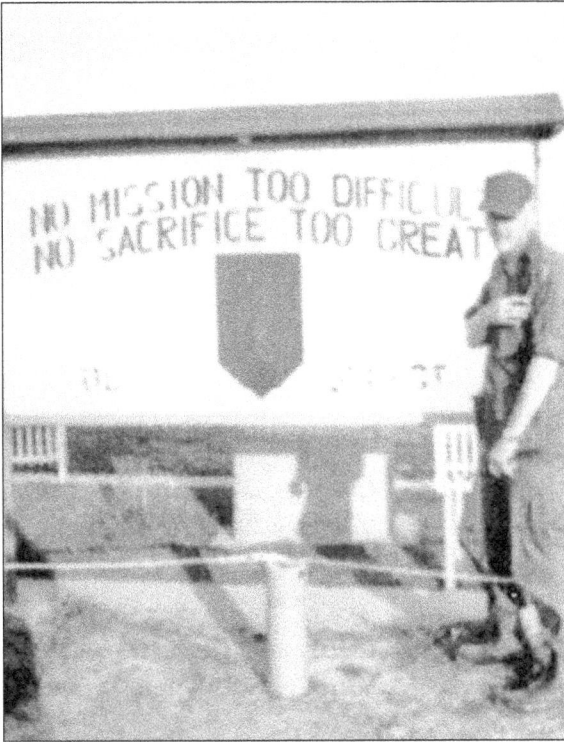

1st Infantry Division Headquarters,
Dian Vietnam, February 1967

you might as well be a Big Red One." We were loaded onto an airplane and flown to Di An, headquarters for the First Infantry Division.

Upon arrival at Division Headquarters, we were greeted by a large sign with the Division crest on it. The words above and below the green crest with the red "1" said "No Mission Too Difficult, No Sacrifice Too Great, Duty First." Who the hell wrote that line of crap? And I still didn't have a damn rifle. What kind of war is this when they won't give me a rifle?

Once in Di An, we were assigned a bunk and I very quickly made myself at home. Although I still didn't know where I was, relative to the war, I was starting to get more comfortable. I was most uncomfortable when I had to take a nighttime stroll out to the piss tubes behind the barracks. I really didn't know how far the perimeter was from the barracks and I could only see open field past the piss tubes. I really didn't want to get anything shot off; after all, I had been married less than two months. It is funny what things go through your mind, and how you set your priorities when you know you are in danger.

It was in Di An that I first met Charles Matthews from Canton, North Carolina. He was assigned to the bunk across the aisle from me. One night he and some of his buddies went to the EM club and had a few too many beers. I later found that Charlie wasn't much of a drinker and he got strange when the booze hit him. He came into the barracks in the middle of the night arguing with his friend and threatening to whip his ass. His buddy finally got him onto the top bunk but not before Charlie had managed to wake up everyone in the barracks. Just as I started to drift back to sleep I heard Charlie start moaning and throwing up. He hadn't bothered to lay out his mattress and was sleeping directly on the springs. When he threw up it went through the springs and on to his buddy below and the arguing started again. Someone came down the aisle and threatened to throw them both out of the barracks and have the MPs take them away. Charlie got real quiet for a few minutes and then insisted on apologizing to everyone in the barracks, one at a time. I guess that is when I started taking a liking to Charlie. You couldn't help but like a man who realized he had offended twenty or thirty guys and wanted to do the right thing by apologizing to each of them, even if it meant pissing them off again. Charlie and I became close friends during our tour in Vietnam and have remained in contact through the years.

The next day we loaded onto planes for Lai Khe. I still didn't know much about the country and imagined that we were going to a small outpost that was in the jungle with only foxholes and makeshift shelters. Before leaving I asked where my rifle was. The clerk laughed and said not to worry I would be getting one soon enough. I imagined being airdropped into a jungle clearing and taking what equipment I needed from the dead or wounded. The DIs at Fort Polk could have done a much better job of preparing us for what to expect. Instead, they took their pleasure in spinning wild tales, much like warriors from past wars had done. The only purpose this initiation served was keeping the new troops mentally alert and scared shitless.

CHAPTER 10

GROUND SURVEILLANCE, (11F40)

After the flight from Di An to Lai Khe, we were put on a truck and taken to the headquarters building for the 2nd Battalion, (Mechanized) 2nd Infantry. Lai Khe was in the middle of a huge rubber tree plantation. The French had settled there many years ago and used the local villagers to harvest the sap from the rubber trees. The trees were set in rows about ten meters apart. I was amazed at how straight the rows of trees were. They went for miles in all directions around Lai Khe. These trees had been put in the perfect military formation. You could see straight lines; front to back, left to right, or in diagonals. There were several magnificent French buildings located in Lai Khe, along with an Olympic-size swimming pool. The Americans were using many of the buildings as headquarters and administration buildings. The Americans also operated a hospital in one of the larger buildings. The buildings were very ornate with tile floors and walkways. The windows were very large and could be closed off with heavy wooden shutters. The plantation houses were being used to house high-ranking American officers and the officer's club. The swimming pool was located next to the officer's club and was offlimits to NCOs and enlisted men unless it needed cleaning, or there was a party going on. On those special occasions, enlisted men were often brought in to act as waiters and bartenders for the officers. This is normally where the female Red Cross workers (Donut Dollies) and United Service Organizations (USO) entertainers spent their evenings.

While sitting in the orderly room, doing the normal Army "hurry up and wait" routine, we could hear the radio in the background. The unit had been hit by the "Mad Bomber" again. The battalion commander, Decoy 6, was talking to the brigade commander and giving him a damage report. The clerks started telling us stories about the battalion getting hit on a regular basis by a sniper called the "Mad Bomber." Using a rocket-propelled grenade (RPG7), the sniper picked the day and time he wanted to attack. He waited until the battalion was moving and picked his target very carefully. He only fired once and he never missed. He had been the battalion's constant companion since shortly after they became mechanized. He was the primary reason the battalion changed their call sign from "Decoy" to "Daring."

Charlie and I were assigned to the ground surveillance section. Neither of us had any idea what that was and our inquiries to the clerks came up without an answer. We were instructed how to get to the ground surveillance barracks and we picked up our gear and started down the road. On the way to the barracks, we passed a sign beside the road that read: "Welcome to Decoy, 2nd Battalion (Mech.), 2nd Infantry." It had the division crest and the 2nd Infantry crest on either side of the wording.

Once in the barracks, we were greeted by SSGT Able, the Section Sergeant. SSGT Able pointed to some empty bunks and told us to make ourselves at home. Once we got our gear stowed he would talk to us and send us over to supply to pick up a few things we would be needing. At last, I was going to get a rifle! There were no footlockers so it didn't take long to drop my duffel bag on the floor and unfold my mattress. The mattress smelled like hell. It was rain-soaked, mildewed, and covered with a thick layer of red dust. I walked back to SSGT Able's bunk to get further instructions and he was asleep in his lawn chair. Charlie walked over and we were discussing whether we should wake him up when he suddenly opened his eyes and started talking to us. He slowly got up from the chair, put on his shirt and cap, and took us over to the supply hut to get our rifles, flak jackets, blankets, etc. As we walked back to the barracks I told him we didn't have footlockers and the mattresses were in bad shape. He told us we would have to buy our own footlockers from guys who were going home or go to the village and pick one up. The mattresses were all they had to offer but we could buy a Vietnamese mattress at the village and put over the top of that one. We put our stuff in the barracks and he took us to the village.

The Army base was built around the village of Lai Khe. The village was divided into two sections. There was the "off-limits" section where the Vietnamese people lived, worked, and went to school, and there was the "on-limits" section that had shops, bars, and whorehouses. We went to several shops and SSGT Able taught us how to bargain with the shopkeepers. Although the prices seemed cheap, Able told us that we should never pay the asking price. By the time he was through bargaining with the shopkeeper, she was calling him names and selling him the goods for less than half the original asking price. As we were leaving, the old woman shouted to Able "You fuck you muther don't come back to my shop no more." This was our first introduction to the love/hate relationship that the Vietnamese had with the Americans. This shop became the first stop for all the ground surveillance members when we went to the village. I soon found out that the old woman liked to argue with Americans and always told us not to come back anymore. One day I bought a doll for my wife from another shop before wandering over to the old woman's shop for a cold drink. When she saw the doll, she wanted to know how much I paid for it and where I bought it. She said I had paid too much for it and grabbed my hand and took me back to the shop. She started a yelling match with the shop owner and before long she was giving me some of my money back. It wasn't much but for this old woman, it was the principle of the thing. We went back to her shop and she told us all that, from now on, we were to check with her before we spent our money in the village. When we were back in Lai Khe from the field we always went to her shop first for a cold soda. It was the closest thing to being back home we were going to see for a long time.

During our first week in Lai Khe, we were sent to Jungle School. When I was finally issued a rifle, it was an M14AR. It was like the M14 rifles I had been issued in basic training and in AIT except this one had a switch on the side. I could move the switch and turn the rifle into a fully automatic weapon. I was shown how to do it in Jungle School and warned not to use the fully automatic selection inside the Lai Khe perimeter. Jungle School took about a week and it was held inside the Lai Khe perimeter. There was a rifle range where we sighted in our new rifles, fired M79 grenade launchers, M72 Rocket Launchers, and experimented with several types of explosives like Flex-X and detonation cord. When I got my turn on the rifle range I put the M14AR through its paces. I didn't flip the switch to fully automatic but I did give the trigger a quick workout. The magazines I was issued were full of mud. The M14AR ran through the ammo without missing a lick. As I fired I could see dirt and debris flying out the top of the rifle along with the shell casings. I had heard several stories about how unreliable the M16s were and how soldiers were being killed while trying to clear a jam during a firefight. I was convinced that I wanted to carry the M14AR even if it was heavier than the M16. After all, a guy's life is worth a little sacrifice. There was a large thick jungle area that we patrolled through to learn what the jungle was going to be like. They sure as hell didn't have anything that even came close to this at Fort Polk. After a week we were sent back to our duty assignments and told to get ready to join the battalion in the field. The ground surveillance section was split into two teams when we got there, and with the addition of the new guys Able split the section into four teams. He planned to keep two teams in the field while the other two teams stayed in the rear taking turns on listening post (LP) duty. This was the best news I had heard since I got my orders for Vietnam. Since I had the M14AR I was put on one of the base camp teams. I wasn't allowed to go to the field until I had been issued an M16. They didn't keep M14 ammo in the field and therefore it wasn't allowed in the field. This caused one of those mixed emotion things. The M14AR was great but it wouldn't do much good if I couldn't get ammo for it when I needed it most.

For the first couple of weeks in ground surveillance, I stayed in the rear, pulling LP duty every other night. Charlie and I were assigned to SGT David Hutton's team. Hutton was a career soldier whose parents lived in Indianapolis, within a few blocks of where I lived before getting drafted. When we pulled LP duty we had the next morning off to sleep. After lunch, we went to the motor pool to do preventative maintenance (PM) on the Jeeps for a couple of hours and then to the village for a cold drink, and to practice our Vietnamese and our bargaining techniques. I would go into a shop and bargain them down on something I had no intention of buying, just to see how low they would go. I really developed a knack for pissing off the shop owners.

When we had LP duty we always set up in a guard tower built by the French years before the Americans got involved in the war. The guard tower was outside the perimeter about three hundred meters, on the north side of the Soui Ba Lang Stream. The stream came in on the northeast side of Lai Khe, turned south, and ran around the west side of the village. We often went out early to wash the Jeep and swim in the stream before going on duty. Swimming in the stream was prohibited but if we looked like we were cleaning military equipment no one said much about it. Highway 13, also known as Thunder Road, crossed the stream on a steel bridge next to the guard tower.

The tower had three levels. The biggest rats I have ever seen inhabited the lower level. We set up the ground surveillance radar unit on the second level and a rifle squad took the top level. Most nights passed very quietly and we took turns on

Setting up radar in French guard tower on
northside of Lai Khe, February 1967

the radar, scanning the valley between the stream and the
perimeter.

Lai Khe had at least one Viet Cong sniper assigned to
provide harassment fire on a random basis. On several
occasions, he had picked the guard tower as his target. As far
as people could remember, the sniper had never hit anyone.
He normally fired one or two shots and went away. Whenever
he made his random attacks the whole perimeter would be
put on alert for the rest of the night. On several occasions, the
entire base camp was awakened and had to man positions
until the all clear was sounded. We figured he was one of the
villagers who got a ration of two rounds per month just to keep

us on our toes. After he fired them he crawled back into the village and was fast asleep long before we were. This suspicion was confirmed about six months into my tour of duty. One night the sniper fired and a GI happened to be sighting down his M60 machine gun in the direction of the muzzle flash. The GI opened fire in the general direction and the next day they recovered the body of the sniper. He was a barber from the village and had cut my hair several times.

We ran the radar by attaching it to the batteries on the Jeep. Several times during the night we would shut down the radar and climb off the tower to start the Jeep and recharge the batteries. On more than one occasion the rats in the lower level of the tower came out and made advances on the person as they were climbing up or down from the tower. One night we went to the tower to set up. We got there early and took a swim. When we got the radar into the tower and set it up it was just starting to get dark. Hutton had stayed on the ground to connect the radar to the Jeep. As he started back to the tower one of the rats came running across the steel bridge toward him. He raised his M16 and squeezed off a couple of rounds at the rat. The rounds ricocheted off the bridge and went into the perimeter. Within only a few seconds we were getting return fire from two positions on the perimeter. Almost as soon as the shooting started, the rifle squad leader was on the radio calling for a cease-fire. It was miraculous that no one was hurt, not even the rat.

Highway 13 ran through Lai Khe and was a major trading route for trucks heading for Saigon. At dusk, the traffic was stopped at the top of the hill and stayed there until morning. One night we were awakened when the sentries spotted several small fires burning around the trucks parked on the hill. The rifle squad leader called in the activity and the officer of the day (OD) instructed them to fire a few rounds over their heads to warn them to put the fires out. Signal fires were sometimes used by the Viet Cong to line up targets for mortar teams. The rifle squad fired two shots in the direction of the trucks and the fires were put out. About an hour later the fires started again and once again warning shots were fired in the direction of the trucks. This time the fires did not go out. The OD came over the radio and told us to open fire on the trucks. I laid my M14AR on the ledge of the bunker and flipped the switch to fully automatic. I took out two extra magazines and laid them on the ledge. When the shooting started I held the M14 down on the ledge with one hand and started working the trigger with the other. I tried to squeeze off two and three round bursts but it was hard to control. I emptied the first magazine and popped in the second. To hell with fire discipline, I wanted to see what this bad boy would do. I pulled the trigger down and held it until the magazine was empty. I watched as the tracer rounds found their target and danced into the air after hitting the front of a truck. I quickly put in the third magazine and repeated the action. Before I got through the third magazine the OD was on the radio screaming about exercising fire control on that M60 out there. I went back to the two and three round bursts until the third magazine was empty. By that time the fires were out and the OD was calling for a cease-fire. The fires didn't appear again and after the high wore off, we all settled down for a little shut-eye. Shortly following that night, they took my M14AR away and gave me an M16.

CHAPTER 11

THE GUYS IN THE BAND

Charles Matthews, David Mackaravitz, Robert Warren, and I arrived in country during the first part of February 1967. We were assigned to the ground surveillance section on the same day and became the FNGs of the section. The section was made of people with a wide range of backgrounds, education, and experience. Altogether, we made up what I will call, "the guys in the band."

SSGT Able was a career soldier from West Virginia. He was a quiet man and kept mostly to himself. He very seldom talked about his family or his hometown. It was hard to understand how he managed to get a tour in Vietnam because he had sleeping sickness. You could be carrying on a conversation with him and if he was sitting in a chair, he would drop into a deep sleep. Then, just as suddenly as he went to sleep he would come out of it, look at you for a few seconds, and try to resume the conversation as if nothing had happened. We learned to stop talking when he went to sleep so he didn't miss too much of the conversation. Most of the time I would just walk away and let him sleep. If it was important to me, I would go back when he woke up and finish the conversation. If it wasn't important, I would just drop it and let him initiate the conversation, which he very seldom did. The Commanding Officer (CO) didn't send Able to the field much because of the sickness. Irving Little told me that Able had fallen asleep one

Ground Surveillance Section, Phu Loi, May 1967

day while Irving was driving him around the compound. Irving stopped the Jeep and strapped Able in to keep him from falling out during turns. Able didn't wake up until they were back at the barracks.

SGT Gregory was another career soldier from Puerto Rico. On our first day in ground surveillance, Charlie asked Gregory what it was like to be in the section. Gregory got a very serious look on his face and slowly shook his head and said, "It is very bad. Very, very bad." That was enough to scare the shit out of Charlie. Gregory was gung-ho and wanted to be in a line company looking for the enemy. He didn't get along very well with the other team leaders and within a few months, he was transferred to a line company where he could fulfill his wildest warrior dreams. He always carried a machete and got upset if anyone touched it. He saw it as the ultimate killing weapon.

SGT David Hutton was a career soldier from Indianapolis, Indiana. His parents lived within a couple of blocks of where I lived before I got drafted. Hutton loved to read and always had a stack of books nearby. He was willing to do just about anything for anyone in the section. When we were in the rear he loved to go to the NCO club for gambling and drinking and he closed it down almost every night. When we were in the field he was all business and you couldn't get him to touch alcohol. He was my first team leader in ground surveillance and any time we were working with SGT Hutton, we were well taken care of. While in the field he attended the daily briefings and afterward would bring in a large plastic bag with our share of the daily sundry packs. These were the comfort items that you couldn't buy in the field. Things like toilet paper, writing paper, cigarettes, cigars, candy, etc. It always seemed like we were getting more than our fair share of those items when Hutton brought them in. Outside of the obvious necessities, my favorites were Chuckles candy and White Owl small cigars. Although I didn't smoke, they were great for keeping mosquitos away. After I got out of the service, I looked up Hutton's parents and had a short visit with them. I would call them occasionally just to see how Hutton was doing and where he was stationed. He was stationed in Korea for a while where he got married to a Korean lady named Kim. I think she stayed with his parents in Indianapolis while he was stationed in Germany. Many years after my tour in Vietnam I managed to get in touch with SGT Hutton. We arranged to meet at a reunion and rekindled our friendship. He now lives in Las Vegas, Nevada and to this day I stay in touch with him on a regular basis.

SGT Roy "Red" Butler from Tennessee was another lifer. He loved to drink no matter where he was. If he couldn't get real booze he went to the medics and got cough syrup with alcohol in it to tide him over until he could get to the real stuff. Butler was a short slim man with a red complexion. He liked to pick on certain people and one of those turned out to be more than he could handle. He had turned his wrath towards PFC Walters and Walters wasn't going to let Butler get the best of him. Once, when we were all back in the rear, Butler had been on Walters' ass all day while we were pulling duty at the motor pool. After dinner, Butler went to the NCO club to get drunk. While he was gone Walters opened a CS grenade and put the powder in Butler's towel. Butler always washed his face before he went to bed so it was a sure bet as to what was going to happen. Around 1:00 A.M. we were all awakened by Butler's screams of pain. As usual, he had returned from the NCO club and washed his face. When he dried his face with the towel he rubbed the CS powder all over his face and into both eyes. The moisture made it react quicker. His first reaction was to start splashing water in his face to get it off but that only made it worse. Although he knew who did it, he had no proof and no one would rat on Walters. Butler was a much more agreeable person following that incident. After Walters left the section, Butler turned his attention to Mathews. That too was a mistake!

Corporal Rosser Knee was from New Mexico. He also was a very kind-hearted person. He used to make comments about the prostitutes in the bars and how he felt sorry for what they had to go through. Knee was one of the first members of the section to rotate back to the states after I joined, so, I didn't get to know him very well until I moved back to New Mexico in 2008.

PFC Irving "Dum Dum" Little was from California. His dad was a career Navy man but Irving wanted nothing to do with a career in the military. Irving's dad was a doctor and was one step below an Admiral. Irving had gotten married a year or two before he came to Vietnam. His wife used to write to him and talk about how sad it would be if something happened to Irving and she didn't have a son to remember him by. Irving met his wife in Hawaii on R&R with a mission of getting that family started. When he came back he was on top of the world because he was certain that he had accomplished his mission. A couple of months later he got a letter from his wife confirming his feelings. Irving was a tall muscular man with a great sense of humor. No matter what was going on we could count on Dum-Dum to find the lighter side of the situation and get us all laughing. He got his nickname Dum-Dum from the song about Big "Dum-Dum" Irving, the 142nd fastest gun in the west. During Operation Cedar Falls, Irving found some Viet Cong punji stakes that hadn't been used. He put them in his waterproof bag to bring them back as souvenirs. SGT Gregory sat on the bag and ran one of the punji stakes into his buttocks. He was so enraged that he ripped open the bag with his machete and threw the punji stakes away. When Irving tried to pick them up Gregory threatened to use the machete on him. Gregory and Irving were not the best of friends after that.

PFC Billy R. "Reb" Hennard was from Tennessee. Reb was a likable guy but was selective on who got into his circle of friends. Reb didn't have much use for any of the new guys and made sure he was teamed with the older members of the section when he had to pull field duty. Reb was the second person in the section to go back to the states after I joined the unit.

PFC Roger Comeaux came from somewhere in Louisiana. He used to laugh that his hometown was so far back in the sticks they had to pump in sunshine, and often remarked that the mail was delivered on the backs of swamp turtles. Comeaux was a black man with lots of old world superstitions. He was one of the kindest and gentlest men I have ever known. He never had anything bad to say about anyone and was always willing to help others. The only time he ever took off his uniform, boots, and helmet was to take a quick shower. Even when we were in base camp, he slept fully clothed with his weapon in his bunk. He would untie his boots to get circulation to his feet but he would not take them off. He carried more than his share of ammunition and he cleaned and oiled each round and every magazine daily. If you happened to leave a bandoleer of M16 rounds laying around for more than a couple of days it would disappear. If you asked Comeaux to return it he would always say that he found it laying around not being used, but, would reluctantly give it back, cleaner than when he picked it up. Comeaux said he carried all that ammo because he was planning on going home and didn't want to take a chance on dying just because he ran out of bullets. Comeaux kept a diary and said he was going to write a book about the war someday. I noticed him looking at me one day and writing in his diary. When I asked him what he was writing he said it was about me but would not say what it was. He had sections in his diary on everyone in the outfit but he never shared it with anyone.

PFC Richard Myers was from Delaware. Richie had been in country for over four months when I arrived. He had a degree in chemistry and was offered a job in chemical warfare. He probably would have been given a commission but his attitude was that the Army hadn't paid for any of his education and he was not going to let them use it. He very seldom bathed even when we were in the rear. He looked down on most of us because we had not graduated from college, therefore we could not possibly be on the same level as him. On more than one occasion I locked horns with Richie over some stupid order he had given. It was never serious but it really got under his skin that anyone without a degree would question his judgment. He constantly referred to Charlie as a "narrow-minded Southern bigot." I never saw Charlie do anything to deserve those comments but he just let the comment roll off his back and said, "Boys, you just gotta consider the source."

PFC Dominic Mish was from East Chicago, Indiana. Mish was another of those short-timers when I joined the section. He was a great guy and friendly to everyone. About nine months into his tour he got tired of the constant bickering between SGT Butler, SGT Gregory, and SGT Hutton and he left the section to join the Reconnaissance Platoon. Within a month he was wounded in his right hand and sent back to the states. Prior to being drafted, Mish had a promising career in football. Although he had been recruited to play college football he was drafted into the Army before he could get enrolled. The hand wound pretty much ended his chances of playing football.

PFC Garcia was from Texas. I didn't get to know him very well before he left the section and became the Company Mail Clerk. Garcia got tired of the bickering between Hutton, Butler, and Gregory and joined Recon along with Mish. While riding on top of an APC a piece of shrapnel went through his helmet and into his left ear. When he came back from the hospital he refused to go back to the field so they gave him a job as the Mail Clerk.

PFC Robert Warren was from Brooklyn, New York. Bob was very laid back and took most things in stride. He had a thick Brooklyn accent and got along well with everyone. Bob's role many times was to be the negotiator when two guys found it tough to get along. He had a knack for getting between them and helping to resolve most issues. He would have been well suited to sit at the negotiation table in Paris during the peace talks that never seemed to get underway. Bob's dad worked as a stagehand in one of the theaters in Manhattan. He used to talk about the gang back in Brooklyn and the neighborhood bar he hung out in before he was drafted. He made New York seem like a great place to live.

PFC David Mackaravitz was from Pennsylvania. Mackaravitz was Polish and not exactly the brightest guy in the outfit. When he and I were in AIT he dropped a mortar round in the tube upside down. The instructors cleared the area and gave him instructions on how to get it out. They left him in the mortar pit by himself to get the round out. He dumped it out of the tube onto the ground and picked it up and started waving it around. He didn't change much when we got to Vietnam. While cleaning his weapon one morning, Mackaravitz almost shot me in the head. The procedure was to remove the magazine, pull the charging handle to clear the round from the chamber, and then pull the trigger. Mackaravitz removed the round from the chamber but forgot to take out the magazine before he did it so he just put another round in the chamber. He then removed the magazine and pulled the trigger, firing the round. The muzzle was right next to my head and the muzzle flash burned my hair. Although I was really pissed, my ears were ringing and my scalp was burning, so I didn't go after Mackaravitz. Before our tour of duty was over Mackaravitz volunteered for door gunner duty and extended his tour in Vietnam.

We had several other guys join the section later during my tour. Three or four months into my tour a guy from Ohio named Ed Dale joined our little group for a while. On his first day in the outfit, we gave him a proper initiation. As he sat in the center of the barracks talking with some of the guys, Charlie and I plotted his initiation. I took out a dud hand grenade and gave it to Charlie. Charlie acted like he was drunk and we got into an argument. He was yelling at me and threatening to kill me if I didn't do what he was asking me to do. I told him to fuck off and walked down to join the group sitting on the bunks talking to Ed. I sat there for about five minutes when Charlie came down the aisle with the hand grenade. He started threatening me again and I reached out to take the grenade from him. Instead of grabbing the grenade I stuck my finger through the ring and pulled the pin out of the grenade. As the handle went flying, I could see Ed's eyes getting bigger and bigger. People started yelling and rolling off the bunks and Ed jumped over the bunk in front of him and ran out the door. We were literally rolling in the aisles with laughter when he went out the door. Once outside he heard the laughter, and no explosion, and turned to see what was going on. When we got him back inside and calmed down we all welcomed him to the outfit and headed down to the EM club for a beer.

PFC Charles Matthews was from North Carolina. I have already written about Charlie in earlier chapters of this book but didn't want to leave him out of the band.

PFC Walters joined our little group shortly after Ed Dale. Walters was from Arizona and came to us with many talents. He had worked in the armory and loved to take weapons apart and work on them. Walters had a thing for Viet Cong hand grenades. Those grenades were so unpredictable that most people wouldn't even pick them up. Walters loved to take them apart, work on them, and put them back together. He even carried a few of them with him when he went to the field. Another talent Walters had was breathing fire. He would squirt cigarette lighter fluid in his mouth and blow it out across a burning lighter. He could make a ball of fire about five to six feet in diameter. We decided to have some fun one night and

MY WAR AND WELCOME TO IT

went over to the cooks' and clerks' barracks. Walters loaded up outside the barracks and Charlie and I ran in screaming "Incoming." Walters ignited the fireball and the barracks started to empty as the cooks and clerks ran outside and dove into their bunkers. It had been raining and the bunkers were wet and muddy. The guys were pissed but laughed it off. We had a beer and decided to give it a try outside the bachelor officer's quarters (BOQ). We snuck over in the dark and Walters loaded up. Just as we were ready to yell "Incoming," Walters thought about how funny this was going to be and started to laugh. When he tried to laugh, he swallowed the lighter fluid and started to gag. We took him back to the barracks and washed down the lighter fluid with beer. He got sicker than a dog and threw up several times. It was a long time before we could talk him into that stunt again.

The next two guys to join our group were Specialists Fourth Class Richard Ducat, from Kankakee, Illinois and Allen Green, from New Orleans, Louisiana. Both men were transferred from stateside duty to Vietnam when it was discovered that they had slightly less than a year to go in the Army. As I recall, they were stationed somewhere on the West Coast when they got their orders. They both had a short leave at home and were shipped to Vietnam. They only had eight to ten months left in the service when they got to our unit.

Although they were both black men from Louisiana, Roger Comeaux never got along with Allen Green. Green came from New Orleans and to put in Roger's words, "Green has those big city ways that I just don't care for." I think Green was the first guy in our section to openly smoke pot. We knew when he had been smoking it because he would stare off into the distance and start singing in a high voice. One time he and Charlie had stayed in the rear while the rest of the unit was in the field. Charlie was cleaning the barracks and Green was sitting on his bunk smoking pot. He hadn't said a word for a long time and then out of the blue he looked at Charlie and said, "Charlie. Come fly with me." He then rolled off the bunk backward and passed out.

Gary Tiegers was from California and had been in Vietnam once before. When he got out of the service he was required to do his time in the Reserves. After a couple of years of attending weekend meetings and two weeks of summer camp, he volunteered to return to Vietnam to complete his military obligation. During his first tour, he was with a leg unit of the Big Red One and came fully prepared to carry everything on his back. Although we were a mechanized unit and there was no need to use a backpack, Tiegers was never seen without his backpack full of stuff. He also had a knack for acquiring things. Within a few days of joining our unit, he came into the barracks with an AK-47 and a .45 caliber grease gun. The grease gun was brand new and covered with packing grease. He was constantly trading with someone and bringing in new stuff.

SGT David Marquin was transferred into our section from another company. He was trying to get promoted and thought an extended tour in Vietnam was the quickest way to do it. He put in for an extension and a thirty-day leave. He flew to Hawaii to meet his girlfriend and they got married. When he came back from his honeymoon, he assumed command of the ground surveillance section from me because he had more time in grade than I did. Marquin and I didn't get along at all. In fact, Marquin didn't get along with a lot of people. He tried to force us to eat all the C rations, not just the "good" stuff. For months we had been picking through the C rations and breaking open the cartons and taking what we wanted and leaving the rest. Eventually, most of the rations were eaten or given to kids in the villages. Marquin decided that we were going to eat the rations in a military style. He would issue them to us and we were stuck with what he pulled out of the box. This went on for about a week before we started raiding the C rations at night and taking what we wanted. He blamed me for this and I gladly took the blame and explained to him that he was going to get tired of trying to stay awake twenty-four hours a day to guard those C rations. He also insisted that we clean our weapons in the predawn hours before stand too. Attempts to clean a rifle in the dark are futile. Because of this we sometimes failed weapons inspection, and Marquin got the blame for that. Not to mention that it didn't make a lot of sense to take your weapon apart just before the sun came up. The Viet Cong (VC) were known to mount attacks on unsuspecting units that were trying to get in a little breakfast before starting the day's activities.

While I was working on Marquin from the angle of being a real pain in the ass, Charlie was working on him from a different angle. Marquin would pass around letters from his wife for the rest of us to read. These were the kinds of letters that were meant to be shared between a man and a woman, and then destroyed. She talked openly about sex, how she missed him and what she was going to do to him when he came home. Some of the letters were very graphic and left little to the imagination. There were always tearstains on the letters and pleas for Marquin to come home as soon as possible. Charlie started telling Marquin how much this woman loved him and how much she would miss him if something were to happen to him. When Charlie found out that Marquin hadn't signed the extension papers yet he really started pouring it on. After a month of Charlie's psychological warfare, and the crap he was getting from the rest of the section, Marquin decided to forget the extension and go home to his wife. Once again, the section was in my hands and back to normal.

Specialist Fourth Class Roger Bowman, from Seattle, Washington came to us in the fall of 1967. Although there really isn't a fall in Vietnam, we knew it was fall because the World Series was being played back in the States. Bowman was a veteran of the invasion of the Dominican Republic. He came into the section telling "war stories" about his tour in the Dominican Republic. Because of that, he didn't get off to a very good start with the rest of the guys. By the time he arrived, most of us were starting to consider ourselves as short timers. Although we had four or five months to go, we didn't want some FNG telling us how to fight a war. It took several weeks, but his stories eventually died down and he was accepted into the group. Bowman carried around pictures of a Pontiac GTO that he had picked up in the PX at Long Binh. Car manufacturers were selling cars to departing GIs at "straight from the factory prices" and he was going to order a GTO before he left.

SGT Steven York came to us from Connecticut. He had graduated from college and joined the Army. During his tour in Germany, he decided that he wanted to make a career out of the Army. He came from a very well-off family. Shortly after he arrived his dad sent pictures of his new wife. York came to Vietnam straight from Germany but had met his prospective new stepmother when his dad brought her to Germany. I didn't get to know York very well because I left shortly after he got there. He had some crazy ideas about putting the radar units in towers in the field just like they did in Germany. We had a significant disagreement about how to deploy the radar units and I demanded that we split the section into two groups. He could take the new guys and use them however he saw fit, and I would take the guys I had spent the last several months with and make sure they left Vietnam in one piece. I heard through the grapevine that several guys had been wounded when the Viet Cong put an RPG7 into one of the radar towers.

CHAPTER 12

ENTERTAINMENT

When I arrived in the 2nd/2nd the Battalion area was fairly new. There weren't many facilities for enjoying a little downtime. There was a nice officers club next to the mess hall and the BOQ. The NCO club was being built near the battalion headquarters, and the enlisted men had a club in a general purpose (GP) medium tent near the motor pool. There were a few tables in the tent and they kept the drinks in barrels of ice water. The bartender often complained of how cold his hand and arm got during the rush hour, but he kept digging all the way to the bottom if he had to. Although the club was just a tent, it commanded respect. Headgear was removed immediately upon entry or everyone in the club was on your ass. Fighting and roughhousing were not allowed or tolerated in the club. A small amount of profanity was tolerated but if a soldier became too loud or vulgar he was immediately escorted out of the club.

Once or twice a week there were movies between the NCO club and the chapel. Everyone brought their own beer and something to sit on but there were a makeshift screen and a barrel to set the projector on. I remember one night we were watching the TV series *Combat* and it started to rain. Even with the best efforts of the projectionist, the rain managed to fall into the light housing of the projector and crack the projection lamp. We all adjourned to our respective clubs and drank until the clubs were out of the night's supply of beverages.

In time, they built a new EM club in place of the tent. It was a great club and turned out to be nicer than the officers club or the NCO club. The movie theater was upgraded by building a small projection room and putting up an honest to goodness outdoor screen. Some bench seats were installed, but not enough to seat everyone when the battalion was back in the area. The projection booth was big enough to protect the projector and the projectionist during the heaviest monsoon downpour. After I made NCO I went to a movie one night that was interrupted by monsoon rain. We all left the theater and went to the clubs. From the NCO club, I could see the theater. The projectionist kept the movie running even after the last soldier left the seats. At times you couldn't make out the picture on the screen but he kept that movie running until it was finished. I figured the projectionist had a nice dry seat and he could see the screen most of the time. Why not stay there in the dry booth and enjoy the show.

On those rare occasions when we were back in the battalion area between missions, the days and nights were much the same. During the day we worked on our equipment, cleaning, and repairing. Sometimes in the afternoon we took the Jeeps and 3/4-ton trucks to the stream and washed them. That was always a good excuse to go swimming. Occasionally we would slip off to the "On Limits" village of Lai Khe to listen to music, drink Vietnamese beer, and eat something that resembled hamburgers and French fries, except for the taste. Most days we were free to do what we wanted after evening chow. Those were the times that we turned to the movies and clubs. Many nights we just sat around the barracks talking, reading mail, and writing letters home.

Once in a great while, the USO brought in a live show. The best one I saw was a group from Australia. The show opened with a comedian telling jokes about Vietnam, Lai Khe, and the military in general. There was a small band with the group but the entertainers who got everyone's attention were three women singers. I remember them talking about the Gold Coast of Australia and envisioning a place that must be the opposite of where we were at the time. The show went on for about an hour and we were all headed back to the barracks and cold showers.

One other time that I was in the rear and there happened to be a USO show featuring Jan Clayton. Ms. Clayton played Timmy's mom on the TV series *Lassie*. There was also an old man who played the piano and tried to tell a few jokes. She sang a few songs, but most of the time was spent just talking to us. There weren't more than a dozen or so GIs there so she kept it very informal and low key. We each spent time talking to her about things we were interested in. When I found out she lived in New Mexico I felt like I had just made a connection straight back to home.

I was back in base camp getting ready to go to Hawaii on R&R when I experienced my third USO tour. Miss America and her court were in Vietnam making the rounds and saying hello to the boys. I had witnessed a Huey flyover of that group just before I left the field. On the day they were coming to have lunch with the 2nd/2nd, Charlie and I debated if it was worth getting cleaned up and going to the mess hall, or just continuing to get ready to leave on R&R. We decided to stick with the latter. After all, what did we need to see those strange girls for when we were going to be reunited with the two most beautiful girls in the world in a couple of days? I got undressed, wrapped a towel around me, slipped into my shower shoes and headed for the shower. The water had been in the tanks long enough to heat up and I was going to get myself a hot shower while the other guys were at chow. After the shower, I toweled off and headed back for the barracks. On the way back, I stepped in some mud and my shower shoe got stuck. As I tried to free it without stepping out of it, a Jeep went by and honked its horn. I turned to look and it was several of the girls from Miss America's court and they were waiving. I instinctively raised my free hand to wave and as I did the towel slipped to the ground around my feet. The girls kept waiving and the Jeep kept moving and I scrambled to cover things up and get back to the barracks.

When it came time for Bob Hope to bring his show to Lai Khe, we packed up and moved out. One of the things that made Vietnam bearable was the chance of getting to see Bob Hope perform live and become a part of history. I had watched the Bob Hope tours on television for as long as I could remember and at long last, I was going to be a part of one of those shows. That was not to be.

CHAPTER 13

VIETNAMESE ANIMALS

No story about Vietnam would be complete without a few good tales about the animals you experience there. One of the things I marveled at while in Vietnam was the different types of animals, bugs, and reptiles I saw.

American soldiers had a love for dogs very much unlike the love the Vietnamese had for them. I remember seeing a Norman Rockwell painting of a boy sharing his lunch with his dog but I don't believe I ever saw a picture that depicted people sharing their dog for lunch. The Vietnamese had a taste for dog and the American soldiers tended to keep stray dogs as pets. Our section had such a dog. The dog's name was "Yeller," and he looked like the dog in the *Old Yeller* movie. Yeller was a muscular dog that liked to hang around with the guys in the Section, and we liked having him around. When we loaded into the Jeep to go for a ride, Yeller was always in the Jeep by the time it was started. He loved to ride on the hood where he looked like an oversized hood ornament for a Mack truck. From that vantage point, he was the "King of The Road." He rode with his head held high as if he were showing off to all the other dogs we passed along the way. He was a strong and proud looking dog but he was afraid of his own shadow. On more than one occasion we had to rescue him from a dog less than half his size, as he was being chased across the compound. Once safely inside the barracks, he

Yeller

quickly regained his composure and became our *Old Yeller* hero again.

My first experience with exotic reptiles in Vietnam came while standing guard duty on the Lai Khe perimeter. SGT Hutton was telling us stories about the "Fuck You" lizards. The story sounded so strange that we thought he was making it up. Then, shortly after sundown, we heard a high-pitched voice in the dark saying, "fuck you, fuck you." We were amazed at the sound but Hutton got spooked and grabbed his rifle. It turned out that although he had heard of the lizards, this was his first time to hear one.

One day while we were working an area suspected to be a resupply area for the VC one of the line company squads came upon a large boa constrictor. As it slithered through the tall grass the guys on the ground were scattering to get away from it. The APC driver gave chase and they managed to shoot it with the 50-caliber machine gun. When the shooting started everyone in the area went on alert until we were informed that they had taken a prisoner and were dragging it back to the night defensive position (NDP). That comment caused several of the commanders to question just what the hell was going on. When they pulled the snake into the perimeter we all gathered around to look at it. It was the biggest snake I had ever seen. Several months later we were asked to hunt for a boa that had crawled into a small hamlet and taken a baby off his sleeping mat. Seems like this wasn't the first time this had happened and the snake was never found. We also heard stories of rats that would run in packs and attack babies and small dogs.

The snake most feared by me was the one they called the one-step snake. I never saw one but I did hear stories about them and had no desire to even come close to them. I did see a woman that was bitten by one in our battalion area one day. She was one of the Vietnamese workers hired by Pacific Architects and Engineers to pick up trash in the area. One of the American soldiers who witnessed it said she was bending down picking up trash when she suddenly screamed and turned to run away but only made a few steps before she went down. When he got over to her she was foaming at the mouth and convulsing. A few others joined him to look for the snake but there was nothing they could do for her. He said the snake wasn't very big but it packed a powerful venom.

One day while I was laying on the ground to provide road security for a passing convoy I noticed very colorful bugs crawling around me. They were unlike any bugs I had ever seen and I can't start to describe them here but they were the brightest reds and blues I had ever seen on bugs. After that day I paid a little more attention to what was crawling around on the ground. To this day I have never seen anything that looks like the bugs I saw in Vietnam.

I had two monkeys while I was in Vietnam. The first one was given to me one morning while I was on a water run in Lai Khe. The guy in the next Jeep had a monkey climbing around all over the Jeep. I held out my hand and the monkey came right to me. As we sat in line for water I played with the monkey. The guy told me he was going home soon and asked if I would like to have her. I said yes never thinking about how I was going to take care of a monkey. When I got back to the barracks SGT Able ask me where I got the monkey. He started playing with her and much to my surprise told me I could keep her if I wanted to take the responsibility. He had a monkey when he first arrived in Vietnam and the guys in the section took turns taking care of it. Rosser Knee took it on perimeter duty with him one night and during the night their bunker was hit by a mortar round. The concussion caused a hearing problem for Rosser and it killed the monkey. SGT Able was so pissed about the monkey that he never even asked about Rosser's hearing problem. There were still hard feelings about the monkey when Rosser went home.

I named my monkey "Irma La Douce" for the character in the movie. Irma soon became the section mascot and went everywhere we went. During the trips to the field, she would sit on my shoulder and hang on to the hair on the back of my head for support. I managed to buy bananas and nuts from villagers and kept them in a large ammo can. When we were in the jungle Irma got scared at night and would sit on the lap of the person running the radar unit. She would lay on her belly on my leg with her legs and arms firmly wrapped around my leg. If I suddenly woke her she would try to bite me. Not a hard bite but just enough to let me know she didn't appreciate having her sleep disturbed. We took turns watching her and feeding her but after a few months, it just got to be too much to handle so I gave her to one of the guys in supply. Charlie harassed me for weeks about being a flesh trader and wanted to know if that was how I was going to handle the responsibility of kids if I ever had any. Before getting rid of Irma, I took her with me to pick up my laundry one day. The Vietnamese had a fear of monkeys, which as I understood went

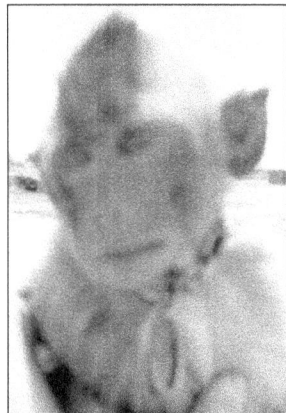

Irma La Douce

back to a time when there was a plague in Vietnam that was spread by monkey bites. While we were in the laundry tent Kim Phi came over and held out a bottle of Coke to Irma. Irma slowly crawled down my arm until she could touch the Coke bottle. She grabbed the neck of the bottle and was looking at Kim Phi when without warning she quickly pulled the bottle to her and bit Kim's hand. All the Vietnamese ladies in the laundry went nuts and started calling me names and told me to get out. After that my laundry bill almost doubled and I got less than friendly service at the laundry tent. It took some time before Kim Phi would talk to me when I dropped off or picked up laundry.

The second monkey I had was not as nice as Irma and wasn't around long enough to get a name, at least not a name that I gave him. For some reason, this monkey hated blacks and Vietnamese. Shortly after I got him he took a bite out of Roger Comeaux and we had to send him off for rabies testing. I turned him over to a medic who was going back to Lai Khe. The medic went to the mess tent to get a bite to eat while waiting on a chopper ride. While he was eating his lunch, the monkey got loose and bit two more black guys who were working in the mess tent. The monkey was quickly put to sleep by the medic's .45 pistol. We were informed later that he didn't have rabies.

CHAPTER 14

PREK LOC II, MY BAPTISM OF FIRE

On March 10, 1967, a ground surveillance team, made up of SGT David Hutton, PFC Tom Copeland, and PFC Charlie Mathews left Lai Khe to relieve the team working with Headquarters and Headquarters Company (HHC) at the Prek Klok II Base Camp. We flew from Lai Khe to Soui Da on a Huey helicopter and transferred to a 2½-ton truck to finish the journey with a resupply convoy to Prek Klok II. Upon arrival, we talked briefly with the departing team and Charlie and I were assigned to a foxhole on the perimeter to stand watch. A few hours later we were taken off guard duty to help fight a fire that had started in a large pile of trees that had been knocked down and pushed into a pile by bulldozers working to clear the base camp. The engineers were building a Special Forces base camp and a runway, and the battalion was there to provide security for the engineers and do search and destroy missions in the area. Using only shovels, Charlie and I tried for several hours to bring the fire under control before the decision was made to let it burn. Thinking back, this was my first major exposure to Agent Orange. The entire area had been heavily sprayed with Agent Orange to strip the trees of leaves and deny the enemy a place to hide. Those burning trees were soaked with Agent Orange. As we were trying to put out the fire we were standing in the smoke. I remember my skin burning, my eyes watering, burning, and itching, and my lungs hurting from the smoke.

Later that afternoon we were assigned to a foxhole located near the command center and told to stand guard there that evening. I developed a sore throat and went to the medics to get it checked out. I was told I had an advanced case of strep throat, given a huge shot of penicillin in my hip, and put on 24-hour bed rest. The doctor who examined me said it was bad enough that I would be sent back to Lai Khe the next morning. I was instructed to go back to my position, lie down, and keep warm. Keep warm? Hell, it was 120 degrees out there, and he was worried about me keeping warm? Soon after I lay down I began to get chills and started shivering. I assume this was a reaction to the shot of penicillin that was so big my entire leg was hurting. It felt like I had been hit with a ball bat just below my right hip. I covered up with a blanket and managed to fall asleep for an hour or so.

After evening chow, I was sitting at the forward position talking with Mathews and Hutton about what we had done on our first day in the field. Just before I went back to my "bed rest" position for the evening I jokingly told Mathews that if the VC came that night he was to tell them to go away because I wasn't feeling well. Around 9:00 P.M. I went back to our daytime position and settled in for the night. The chills had gone away but my leg and throat were still hurting. I had a poncho stretched out between tent poles to lie under and used my helmet for a pillow.

A little after 10:00 P.M. I started hearing explosions coming from the direction of the runway and stuff was falling on my poncho. My first thought was that it had started raining, but I also thought the explosions didn't sound like outgoing artillery rounds, there was something different in the sound. I looked over and saw the explosions coming from the ground and the dirt flying into the air. I grabbed my helmet, rifle, and web gear and dove into the foxhole. I was in there all by myself and I don't mind saying I was scared shitless. I sat down in the very bottom corner of the hole, praying to God, as I looked up and out of the hole. As I sat there the top of the hole appeared to take the shape of a funnel and I just knew mortar rounds were going to start pouring into the hole with me. I decided to move to the forward position with the other guys and just as I was getting out of the hole, I saw a round hit directly in their hole. My heart sunk and I knew they were all dead. Right after the shelling stopped I stuck my head out of the hole to get ready for something, but I didn't know what to expect. The first thing I saw was a large group of shadows running right at my foxhole. My first thought was that the VC had broken through the perimeter and were going after the artillery positions. A thousand thoughts were running through my head as I raised my weapon to start firing. Just as I released the safety I noticed that they were wearing American helmets. It was a group of engineers coming over to secure the runway. They took up positions in the ditch alongside the road. After they moved into the ditch, the flares started coming out and I could see this eerie scene when I looked across the perimeter.

As I was standing up in the hole and looking around I heard a pop-zing sound coming from the direction of the mess tent. I noticed that every time I stood to see what was going on I heard that sound. After the third or fourth time of standing, hearing the pop-zing, I heard one of the engineers calling for a medic. He had been struck by one of the sniper rounds that was meant for me. The first round of flares was dropping below the horizon when the medic came to treat the man.

Shortly after that, a specialist 5th class (SP5) from HHC (I do not remember his name) came by to check on me and told me to stay where I was. He also told me he had just left the other hole and they were all fine. The round had hit just in front of the hole but no one was injured.

I asked him about the pop-zing sound and he told me it sounded like a carbine. The next morning, they found a VC lying next to the mess tent with an M-1 carbine. He had evidently been killed by a stray round. I guess all the praying to God worked for me that night.

Prek Klok II, March 11, 1967

Over two hundred mortar rounds were dropped into the perimeter in less than thirty minutes. No sooner had the mortar attack stopped than the perimeter probes started. Fierce firefights were breaking out all around the perimeter. More flares were hung and choppers started bringing in more ammo and evacuating the wounded. Within an hour we were receiving air support from the Air Force. The artillery fire was pulled back away from the perimeter and the Air Force started making strafing runs between the artillery impact area and the perimeter. Then there was this eerie sound with a stream of red light coming from the sky. Snoopy had moved in and was laying down a hellish field of fire on the retreating enemy. Five thousand rounds per minute, with every fifth round a tracer and it made a steady stream of light and a burrrrrrrpp sound when it fired. This was my first, but not my last, encounter with this wonderful piece of equipment. Since the day I set foot in Vietnam, I was hearing stories about "Snoopy," also called "Puff the Magic Dragon," and now I knew full well what it was.

The ground attack raged on for several hours, but soon after the air power showed up on the scene the enemy started to pull back. We continued to get perimeter probes and sniper fire until around 4:30 A.M.

On the morning of March 11th, Charlie and I were assigned to help police up the VC bodies, put them in the back of a ¾-ton truck, and haul them to the mass grave site. The official count was 197 enemy dead, 3 American dead, and 20 wounded.

On March 12th we started our move back to Lai Khe. We first moved to Soui Da and spent the night at the 3rd Brigade NDP. Those who had been reluctant to dig foxholes in the past were seen digging them deep at Soui Da. On the morning of March 13th, we convoyed through Tay Ninh City, Saigon, and back into Lai Khe. It was sort of a victory lap for the battalion.

CHAPTER 15

NEW DUTIES

After returning to Lai Khe, the ground surveillance section stood down for a while. A four-man team was selected to participate as the Honor Guard for the Change of Command Ceremony transferring command of the 1st Infantry Division from Major General William E. DePuy to General John H. Hay. Since SGT Butler had participated in honor guard duty in his previous assignment, he was selected to head up the team. He selected Irving Little, Richie Myers, and me to complete the four-man team. Butler and Little carried the rifles, Myers carried the American flag, and I carried the Division flag. We practiced for a couple of days to make sure the routine was perfect. On the day of the ceremony, we performed without a hitch. As we marched the flags into position in front of the two generals, I found myself standing face to face with General Hay. I can remember thinking to myself, "Now this man looks like a real general." Like I was some sort of expert. My only other encounter with a general was when I ran smack dab into General Bernard Rogers. I was processing into the 1st Infantry Division in Di An and was put on KP following breakfast one morning. They released me from kitchen patrol (KP) with only a couple of minutes to spare before I had to be at a class for part of the processing. I left the mess hall running in a dead heat so I could make my class on time. As I rounded the corner of a building I collided with General Rogers. The collision caused me to see stars—the stars were on his collar and helmet. I had never been this close to a general before and had almost knocked him down. Nothing good was going to come of this and I figured I would probably be locked up or put in front of a firing squad. Hell, if a DI could kill you for not doing pushups right, what could a general do to you for almost knocking him down? I quickly came to attention and started to give him my best salute. As my hand was going up to my forehead, General Rogers reached out, grabbed my hand, and shook it. He pointed to the name tag on his shirt and said, "Welcome to the 1st Division son. The name is Rogers, Bernie Rogers. If you need anything while you are in Vietnam don't hesitate to let me know." Wow! Instead of making an enemy, I just made a friend. Of course, I never tried to contact him for anything and only saw him, from a distance, once or twice during my tour in Vietnam.

Following the Change of Command, there was talk in the battalion that the four of us on the Honor Guard had done so well that we were going to be transferred to division to become the Division Honor Guard. What an honor that would have been, but it was only a rumor and we soon found ourselves back to doing our daily duties.

During the stand-down, the 2nd Battalion had an awards ceremony for those who participated in the Battle of Prek Klok II. Dave Hutton, Charlie Mathews, and I received our Combat Infantryman's Badges. We were among the first in the ground surveillance section to get the awards.

Prior to the Battle of Prek Klok II, the ground surveillance section had three radar teams, and only one working radar unit. The normal mode of operation was to send one team to the field with HHC while the other two teams stayed in Lai Khe base camp. The one working radar unit was used on the north side of the Lai Khe perimeter every night. We normally set that unit on the second floor of the French Guard Tower that sat beside Highway 13 about a quarter mile outside the perimeter. We would point the radar back towards Lai Khe and sweep the valley along either side of the stream that ran around the north side. Occasionally, we monitored activity along Highway 13 to the North of the guard tower. There was a rifle squad assigned to the top level of the tower as a listening post. At some point, the decision was made to no longer use the tower for these operations, and the radar and rifle squad were moved back onto the Lai Khe perimeter. We still swept the valley along the stream and monitored activity on Highway 13, but it was not as effective, because we no longer had the height of the tower to operate from. That was fine with us because it made us less of a target for RPGs and snipers.

We eventually got all three radar units working and were assigned to various line companies in the battalion. Once that happened we saw very little of our barracks in Lai Khe. On several occasions, we would be assigned to one line company in a position in the field. That line company would move to a new position and a different line company would move into that position to take their place. When that happened, we were often told to stay where we were until the new line company arrived. So there the three of us sat, with a Jeep and trailer waiting for the next company to arrive. There were times when we sat there for several hours waiting for the new company to arrive.

Sometime during the summer of '67, we started having spotlight teams assigned to work alongside us. Many of the company commanders had no idea what the function of the radar or the spotlights were, so, they left it up to us to determine how to position them. On a couple of occasions, we were told by the CO to set up so we could monitor a tree line that was less than fifty meters from our position. The radar had an eighty-meter dead space, so, if we couldn't get the CO to listen to us, we would turn on the radar and let it sweep in auto-mode, take off the headphones and trust our own senses to determine what might be coming out of the woods.

At some point, the battalion received a new electronic monitoring device. It worked by burying a wire loop in the ground outside the perimeter and if someone crossed it carrying metal, it would detect them and set off an alarm. We did a test during daylight hours and could never get it to work properly. The battalion intelligence officer who delivered it to us never came back to see if it was working, so, we just left it in the trailer and depended on the radar.

CHAPTER 16

PHU LOI

During the next few months, April to July, the 2nd/2nd spent a lot of time working in the Phu Loi area. We spent very little time working as a full battalion. One or two line companies were usually operating independently from the battalion. We would rotate in and out of the Aviation base in Phu Loi, often working around Claymore Corner and the Crooked Village. We did Pacification Operations, Medcap Operations, and a few Search and Destroy Operations. Most of the time, when we were trying to "Win the Hearts and Minds" of the civilians, we could win them during the day but the VC and North Vietnamese Army (NVA) had them during the night, and any other time we were not around. When we set up an NDP near the Crooked Village you could bet that sometime during the night we were going to get sniper fire or an occasional RPG from inside the village. On one occasion, ground surveillance was attached to "C" Company. While we were digging in, the company commander made a trip to the village along with the Vietnamese Interpreter. He found the village chief and told him that he should have his people sleep in the bunkers under their beds because, if one shot was fired from the village, in our direction, we were going to level the village. It was a very peaceful night!

In May, the battalion commander's helicopter was shot down one morning as he left the perimeter to direct operations

Near the Crooked Village, 1967

from the air. Our radar unit had broken down during the night and we had received permission to take it to Di An for repairs. As we were standing by the Jeep, waiting for the convoy to form up and head out, the battalion CO came out of his tent and saw us standing there. He came over and asked who was in charge. I saluted him and told him it was me. He said, "Specialist, I don't know who the hell gave you that rank but if you don't get those men busy doing something I am going to rip it off of you!" I explained that we were waiting for the roads to be cleared so we could go to Di An. He said; "I don't give a damn what you are waiting for, get those damn people busy doing something!" Then he turned and walked to his waiting helicopter.

As the helicopter lifted off, we rummaged around trying to look like we were picking up trash. As the helicopter left the perimeter and flew out across the trees there was a loud explosion and the chopper went down. As we watched it go down there were people all around the perimeter who started to applaud. As it went down and disappeared into the jungle below, we could hear him on the radio screaming for someone to come get him because the VC had him surrounded. Keep in mind that he was within walking distance of his Tactical Operation Center (TOC). One of the line companies managed to turn around and pick him up and bring him back into the perimeter. He was unhurt and the chopper pilot had a few scratches. The CO was yelling that he wanted that incompetent SOB court-martialed for getting him shot down. For the rest of the week, he never left the perimeter or the TOC.

There was a Change of Command while we were in the field. When the old CO got into the Huey to be taken out, I saw him talking to the pilot and shaking his finger at him. As the chopper lifted off, it went straight up until it appeared to be a little spec in the sky and then flew off. This was the most hated officer in the battalion during my tour.

As for the broken radar unit, we took it to Di An and dropped it off at the 701st Maintenance trailer. I took it into the trailer and never wanted to leave. This was the only building I was in during my time in Vietnam that had air conditioning. It was very nice in there but I was not allowed to stay. We went to the Tastee Freeze and got in line for ice cream cones. You could only buy one at a time, but you could go to the back of the line and go through as many times as you wanted. We then went to the Vietnamese Beer Garden, just off base, and had a hamburger and French fries. What a break we got that day! Then back to the 701st to pick up the radar and back to the field.

The new Battalion Commander was Lieutenant Colonel John Dew Pelton. What a fantastic guy and 180-degree difference from the old CO. Lt. Colonel Pelton walked the perimeter every night checking on the troops to see if they needed anything. He always had a backpack full of clean dry socks to pass out. What a fantastic thing to do.

He also understood how the radar worked and what it could do for him. One evening he had me set up two radar units on opposite sides of the perimeter. He was "leading" the battalion on a dismounted search and destroy mission. Our job was to use the radar to sweep both sides of the column as they moved between the perimeter and the village. We were left in the perimeter along with the APCs and very few other soldiers while most of the battalion crossed into the village over half a mile away. They surrounded the village and right at dawn they moved in looking for VC. No such luck that night.

CHAPTER 17

OPERATION PAUL BUNYAN

In August we moved east of Bien Hoa, to Tan Uyen, to provide security for the 168th Engineer Battalion as they cleared the Ong Dong Jungle, also known as the Heart-Shaped Jungle. This area had been a VC hiding stronghold for several years. It was rumored that several American patrols had been sent into the area and were never heard from again. It was very dense with a heavy overgrowth canopy. Many attempts to defoliate it with Agent Orange proved to be unsuccessful. Now, the 2nd/2nd, along with the 1st Squadron, 4th Cavalry Regiment (¼ Cav) were going to ride shotgun alongside thirty Rome Plows while they flattened over seventy-seven hundred acres of jungle.

The battalion was split up into several operational units with NDPs, within a few miles of each other. The destruction of the jungle was directed from the air by commanders riding in Light Observation Helicopters (LOHs). There was resistance from the enemy but it was very light and sporadic. As I recall, most injuries were from booby traps and tree limbs.

Before setting up areas of operation in the fallen areas, lots of work had to be done to clear tree trunks and vines from the ground. There were no efforts by the Rome Plows to push the downed trees and brush into piles and for the most part, it was left lying where it fell. Chainsaws, hand saws, and axes were used to clear the fallen trees and brush.

Operation Paul Bunyan, September 1967

The ground surveillance radar was of little use in this area so we stood watch at night and did various details during the day. We mostly helped the engineers unload and carry C-4 explosive. The C-4 was being used to collapse tunnels in the area. Those tunnels were so well fortified that many times the explosive had very little effect in collapsing them. There were command centers, hospitals, mess halls, and even an R&R Center, all located underground. The tunnel complex was so large that bicycles were used for transportation inside the tunnels. Many of those bikes were taken back to Lai Khe for use by GIs on the rare occasions that we were back there. Many articles of interest were found in the tunnels, including a pair of binoculars with the HHC Commander's name on them. They had been taken from his hooch a few months before. There were also US Medic's kits and American canned food and C Rations found in the tunnels.

In return for helping the engineers we were given all the C-4 we wanted to use for heating C rations. SGT Butler oversaw the section during this time and he was scared to death of C-4.

He told us we were not to use the C-4 and ordered us to get rid of it. Butler was lying in his bunk on his stomach when Irving Little lit the corner of a block of C-4 and threw it at the head of Butler's bunk and said, "Per your request, I have thrown it away, sergeant." SGT Butler went ballistic and stormed out of the area. A few minutes later he returned with a couple of engineers with orders to collect all the C-4 and bring it back to the engineering area. We managed to keep some small pieces and use them when Butler was not in the area.

During this operation, Charlie Mathews and I left the field and returned to Lai Khe to prepare for our R&R to Hawaii. A few days after we left, SP5 Joseph Lupo, a Medic from HHC was killed when the APC he was driving hit a bomb buried in the mud in the center of our NDP. Lupo was attached to one of the line companies and had returned to the HHC area to pick up medical supplies to take back to the line company. He was driving on a well-used trail inside the NDP when his APC managed to set the bomb off. That trail had been used daily the entire time we had been set up in that NDP. It was just bad luck that Lupo's APC happened to hit the bomb just right and set it off. The bomb had evidently been dropped a long time ago and buried itself in the mud without going off.

CHAPTER 18

REST AND RECUPERATION, HAWAII

In late August, Charlie Matthews and I came in from the field to prepare for our R&R to Hawaii. We had arranged to meet our wives there. His wife, Rita, was coming from North Carolina, and my wife, Linda, was coming from Indiana. This was a week we had looked forward to almost from the day we arrived in Vietnam.

We got back to Lai Khe a few days before we were to leave on R&R. We thought we could lie around, relax, and wash some of the dirt and grime off before we got on the plane. It didn't work out that way. As soon as the officer of the day (OD) found out we were in our barracks he hunted us down and put us to work. We got assigned to "Sanitation Engineer" duty. In other words, we got to burn shit. Charlie and I would go around to the latrines and pull the half barrels out, put some diesel fuel in them and light them. Once we got them going we would sit under a tree and enjoy the fragrance. There is no other smell quite like that of burning diesel fuel and human shit and I hope I never smell anything like it again. The OD was new in country, and in rank, so we pulled as much wool over his eyes as we could. One day he found Charlie and I sitting under a tree watching the shit burn, and he came over and started chewing us out for not following proper procedure. Now we had been in Vietnam for seven months and this was the first either of us had heard about a "proper" procedure for burning shit. I had to wonder, was this really the subject of a class he had to get a passing grade in to get through Officer Candidate School. He informed me that I was not stirring the diesel fuel into the shit before I lit it, or during the burn. Charlie jumped in and started pulling the wool down by saying: "Sir, I do not understand what you mean, Sir." (We both knew a little about proper military procedure.) As he started explaining it to Charlie, we could see just how green he was, so Charlie asked him to demonstrate the procedure for us so we could make sure we got it straight. Charlie pulled out a fresh half barrel for the OD and poured in the diesel fuel. As the OD mixed the diesel fuel into the shit, explaining his proper procedure, we asked several questions about how to tell if it was properly mixed, and anything else we could come up with. He was very patient as he explained it to us. He then instructed me to light it and continue stirring. I started it burning with some paper but would not stir it. He kept telling me to stir and I kept saying I was afraid I would get burned. Always starting and ending each sentence with "Sir." To convince me that I would not get burned, he took the stick and began to stir the burning pot of shit. Charlie and I were both having a hard time keeping a straight face, and the guys on police detail around us were cracking up. I thanked the lieutenant for his help in teaching me the "proper procedure" as he watched me stir a barrel of burning shit. I don't know if it was the laughing as he walked away that made him realize he had just been had, but whatever it was, he did not come back to check on us again. Charlie and I went back to sitting under the tree watching that black smoke roll into the clear blue sky and thinking about how great it was going to be to see our wives again.

We finally broke loose from the shit-burning details and caught a chopper to Di An. In Di An, we transferred to a Caribou and flew to Long Binh. We spent the night in Long Binh and early the next morning we boarded a 707-jet aircraft to Hawaii. There were packets in the seat pockets telling us how to conduct ourselves while on R&R in Hawaii. After all, we were representing the US Army, and they wanted us to be on our best behavior. The flight to Hawaii was over eleven hours long. Because we crossed the International Dateline, we arrived an hour before we left Vietnam. That made for one hell of a long first day in Hawaii. Our wives met us at the Fort De Russy R&R Center. We had to listen to a fifteen to twenty-minute orientation speech and we were on our own. It is hard to explain the feeling of walking out into the sunshine with the woman you love on your arm after spending seven months in a war zone. I just couldn't believe it was happening. The four of us talked for a few minutes, exchanged hotel information, and made plans to meet a couple of days later. We grabbed taxi cabs and were off to start our R&R. The cab ride to the hotel scared the hell out of me. I hadn't gone that fast in ground transportation in months. When we got to the hotel I gave the cab driver a big tip, (I wasn't accustomed to using real money) and we checked in. Our room wasn't ready so we had to wait in the lobby for a while. I finally insisted that they let us take our bags to the room so we could go out and look around. Once we got into the room we convinced the maid that the room looked fine and she didn't need to vacuum the carpet and clean the bathroom fixtures just for us. Once she was gone we started making up for lost time. All I can say is it didn't take long to make up for seven months apart. We changed into civilian clothes and went to find some real food.

Later that afternoon, we called Charlie and Rita. We decided to meet them near their hotel and go for a walk around Honolulu. We went by the rental car places and picked up our cars and made plans for the next day. By early evening I was getting very tired so we went back to our room. The room had two half beds that could be shoved together to make one full sized bed. The whole time we were there we only used one bed. It was so nice being that close to my wife I never wanted to let her go again.

The door coming into the room had a louvered vent that could be opened full or part way. On each side of the patio doors, there were louvered glass panels that opened the same as the vent on the door. We found that if we opened the vent on the door and the vent next to our bed, we got a beautiful breeze that flowed into the window and out the door. It carried a lovely floral fragrance with it which made the sleeping even better. The shower had a never-ending supply of hot water. I had grown accustomed to bathing with a helmet full of water or showering with two gallons of water that had been warmed in the sun. Now I could just stand under the water as long as I wanted. It was great, except it washed off my tan. That nice brown color I had picked up in Vietnam was mostly laterite dust ground into my skin. What the hell, easy come easy go!

On our second day in Hawaii, we met Charlie and Rita and took a drive around the island. We stopped at a roadside park and walked down to the beach. We were having such great fun there we decided to stay for a while. Charlie and I walked back to the cars and got some towels and suntan lotion and joined the ladies for some relaxation on the beach. We waded into the surf and played in the sand for about two hours before deciding to move on.

When we returned to the cars Charlie noticed that one of the windows on his car was open. Rita had left her purse in the car and someone had broken into the car and taken it. We found the purse in a trash can but most of their money and all their traveler's checks were gone. They didn't have much cash in the purse and they were able to get their money back on the traveler's checks but that incident ruined the trip for them both.

On the third day we split up and each couple went their separate ways. Linda and I drove around the western side of the island and stopped at Sea World for a while. A little farther down the road, we found a beautiful waterfall off the beaten track and sat around for a while talking. We drove back into the city and had a late dinner.

R&R in Hawaii, September 1967

After dinner, we drove out toward Diamond Head and found a secluded beach. We spread a blanket and sat there drinking in the stars and the ocean. Although there was no one around I was scared as hell. For seven months I was accustomed to having a gun near me when it got dark and now I was sitting in the open with no protection. Linda wanted to get romantic but I was very uneasy. I tried to explain how I was feeling to her but she just didn't understand why I couldn't leave the war behind me. While we were discussing my uneasiness, I saw several dark shadows coming out of the water and walking toward us. Four people had been snorkeling along the edge of the beach but we couldn't see them until they stood up. Seeing them come out of the water like that just added to my discomfort so we decided to go back to the hotel.

Linda wanted to drive the car back to the hotel. It was a stick shift and she had never driven anything but an automatic transmission. I got the car out onto the highway and let her get behind the wheel. She made several attempts at taking off but couldn't get the hang of letting out the clutch and pressing down the accelerator in the right sequence. If she managed to get the car rolling without killing the engine, it would start loping and jerking. When she finally got enough speed to change gears, she went into high gear and the loping got worse. We would manage to get the car stopped, which usually killed the engine, and start over again. Just as she was starting to get the hang of it, a State Trooper pulled in behind her with his lights on. When he came up to the car he wanted to know what she had been drinking. I explained that I was trying to teach her to drive a stick shift and he told me to get her off the main road before she hurt someone. That hurt her feelings so bad I couldn't get her to try it again during the whole trip.

For the next few days, we continued to take sightseeing trips around the island, doing all those things that normal tourists do and really enjoying each other's company. We cherished every moment we spent with each other because we knew we only had seven days together and we were going to make the most of it. On our last night in Hawaii, Charlie and Rita came to our hotel and we talked for a while. Charlie and I walked down to the desk so I could request a wake-up call. As we walked I told Charlie that I had been thinking about not going back to Vietnam. I told him that Linda and I had decided to stay in Hawaii for a few years and then go back to Indiana. Although I was only joking with him he was taking me seriously. When he and Rita left he shook my hand and said: "Now Mr. Copeland, I will see your ass on that plane to-morrow, right?" He would not let go of my hand until I assured him I would be there.

After they left, Linda wanted to sit up and talk. She didn't want the night to end and we both thought that was a good way to make it last. Everything went fine until about 4:00 A.M. when we both fell asleep. When the phone rang a 6:00 A.M., I got out of bed and answered it. I then went back to bed and slept very soundly until 8:00, the precise moment my plane was scheduled to leave Hawaii. I woke up in a start and knew my ass was in big trouble. I called Fort De Russy and told them what had happened. They told me not to worry about it, but to get down there as soon as I could. Linda and I met with this nice young lieutenant who gave me the Army's version of what I had just done. Technically I was AWOL and I could either report to duty at Fort De Russy for daily work details until they got me on a plane back to Vietnam, or I could pay for my own plane ticket to Vietnam. Either way, I was going to have to face whatever disciplinary actions my commander decided to hand out once I got back. He then asked how much longer Linda was going to be in Hawaii and told us to go out and enjoy ourselves until she left. My only restriction was that I had to report to the airport every morning and be ready to fill an empty seat when it became available. We continued to enjoy ourselves for a couple more days before Linda left. Once she was gone, I moved into a barracks and they put me to work at the center along with about twenty other guys doing whatever needed to be done. It took me about a week to get on a plane to Vietnam. When I got back, the unit had just left Lai Khe for a field exercise. I was instructed to stay in the company area until the company commander got back. He was coming back in a few days and wanted to talk to me. I thought for sure I would be punished for going AWOL. The day he got back he called me over to his quarters for a "little chat." I was prepared for the worst, but when I got there he started asking me about my R&R. He had come back in to start his R&R in Hawaii and he wanted to know what to expect. We talked for about an hour and I was free to go. As I was leaving he said he had just one more thing to tell me. My promotion to SGT E5 had been approved and I would be getting my orders and a set of stripes within a few days.

A day or two later Charlie was sent back in for some dental work. When he walked into the barracks and saw me he let me have it. He thought for sure I had really gone AWOL and he was afraid to tell anyone about our conversation the night before he left. He had a hard time believing that I had missed the plane by accident.

A few days later the battalion came back into Lai Khe for a week and then we moved out again. As we were sitting in the back of a truck waiting to move out, some kids came along selling Cokes. They wouldn't let us take the bottles on the truck so we had to get off to drink it. I was fully loaded with gear when I jumped off the truck to get a Coke. When I hit the ground, I landed with one foot in the bottom of the drainage ditch and the other on top of it and twisted my back. I was in great pain and was sent to the medics. They gave me drugs and put me on bed rest for a week, and the battalion left without me, again. My week of R&R turned into almost a month without going to the field, and a nice promotion to boot.

CHAPTER 19

THE BATTLE OF ONG THANH, OCTOBER 17, 1967

It was one of those hot, humid, October days in the Republic of South Vietnam. We had moved into an NDP in a heavily wooded area about twelve miles northeast of Lai Khe on Route 240. We were providing security around Fire Base Lorraine II and the artillery battery had the 105s and 155s going night and day. A leg outfit had cleared, and previously occupied the NDP, so it was much smaller than we were accustomed to. To provide room for the APCs we were forced to dig in very close to the tree line. Because of the proximity to the tree line, the radar units were of little use on the perimeter. We used them at night to monitor the road that passed through the perimeter. Occasionally we would pick up movement down the road, but, it always turned out to be a few loose water buffalo or an occasional troop of monkeys. Although other units in the area were having contact with NVA forces, it was relatively quiet in our immediate area of operations. We had patrols around our perimeter all during the day and listening posts and ambush patrols working all through the night but there was no sign of Charlie in our neighborhood.

One morning, about 9:00 P.M., the silence was broken by an incoming RPG exploding right in front of one of the few APCs left on the perimeter from the daily patrols. As I looked across the perimeter I saw a second round come from high in the trees. I called the command center and let them know that I had seen the location of the RPG sniper and was instructed to cross the perimeter and direct fire into the location. As I ran across the perimeter, I couldn't help but hope this was not the start of a full-scale assault. I really didn't want to be standing out in the open if the shit was about to hit the fan. After what seemed like an eternity, I reached the APC that was the target of the RPG rounds and was surprised to see that the sniper had missed with both shots. Charlie usually did a better job with his limited resources. The only damage to the position was to the latrine the squad had constructed with sandbags and ammo boxes. The contents of the latrine were scattered all over the area and the smell was terrible. As I gathered the few troops in the area to direct fire into the tree line, the "no fire" order came down from battalion command. Because of the possible presence of our own patrols in the area, command did not want to chance hitting them with friendly fire. Feeling helpless and angry we sat in dismay while our sniper climbed down the tree and vanished into the jungle.

Daytime training on radar, October 1967

When I returned to my area I had to listen to comments about my "Audie Murphy" style heroics of running across the open while hostile fire was coming into the perimeter. We talked about the stupid command decision for about an hour or so before everybody settled into the routine of cleaning weapons, reading and rereading mail, writing to the folks, and digging through the C rations looking for something different. No matter how hard we looked we never found anything that smacked of mom's home cooking, or for that matter, even came close.

On the morning of October 17th, the artillery units in our firebase provided fire support for the 2nd Battalion 28th Infantry "Black Lions" Regiment, who had run into the 271st Viet Cong Regiment near the Ong Thanh Stream. Many of the soldiers in the 2nd/2nd, were pressed into service humping ammo for the artillery.

The 2nd/28th had walked into the 271st Regiment's base camp and was taking heavy casualties. We found out later that as the 2nd/28th tried to flank what they thought was a patrol size ambush, they were running more and more men into the center of the regimental perimeter and certain death. That action raged on for over four hours with only a handful of men from the 2nd/28th surviving the ordeal without being wounded or killed. I listened to many of the calls for help on the PRC-25 radio I had tuned to the 2nd/28th frequency. Every time the mic was keyed I could hear what can only be described as a cacophony of the sounds of battle in the background. Sometimes it was difficult to make out what was being said.

Although they made several attempts to flank the ambush and to break away from the ambush, they were surrounded and outnumbered by a well dug in force. When the 271st finally broke off contact around noon, the 2nd/28th Battalion Commander and the 1st Brigade Operations Officer were left lying dead on the battlefield along with 132 other dead and wounded officers and men from the battalion. Two Americans were reported as "Missing in Action." Those who were left standing evacuated the area with as many of the wounded as they could carry. As other American units arrived to "mop up" they were too late to join the fight. The jungle was so dense, APCs could not get in there and helicopters would not be able to evacuate the dead until landing zones could be cleared the following day. They gathered as many bodies as they could and put them in a small clearing that would be used for a landing zone the next day. During the night artillery fire was laid into the area to keep enemy forces away from those bodies.

Later that afternoon I had just settled in to listen to the World Series, courtesy of Armed Forces Radio in Saigon, and to try to squeeze in a short nap in preparation for the long night ahead. The PRC25 radio once again crackled to life. One of our patrols had started receiving light weapons fire. The patrol was only about two hundred meters outside the perimeter and we could hear the firefight as it took place. They had run into elements of the 271 VC Regiment as they were leaving the battle of Ong Thanh and heading south. Then the report came in that one of the troops had been hit and they were requesting that the doctor meet them halfway. The guy was losing a lot of blood and the medic needed help. The doctor refused to leave the perimeter, or even to leave the command center, until the man had been brought inside the perimeter. The medic called repeatedly for the doctor as they got closer and closer to the perimeter. Each time the request was refused by the doctor, and as he spoke, we could hear the World Series playing in the background. Once inside the perimeter, it took another fifteen minutes for the doctor to reach the wounded man. By that time, it was too late. The doctor commented to the Medic that he might have been able to save the man's life if they had just gotten him in a little sooner. As he was walking away he commented on how this war was a terrible waste of young men.

That evening I walked over to the communications center to get a new battery for the PRC25. After talking to Sparky about the situation in the world and the lack of mail and hot food, I started back to my area. As I passed by the command center I decided to check in for reports on enemy movements in the area. As I walked up to the command center I could hear the World Series still coming over the radio. Then my heart stopped and I felt very sick, there on the ground in front of me, was the man who had died only a short time ago. I had seen dead men before but this was the first time that it had affected me this way. As I stood there looking at the lifeless body, covered with the green poncho, the outside world began to slowly fade away. For a few short minutes, my whole world became totally engulfed by the sounds of the World Series and the sight of this lifeless form, the body of a man who I had never known, but suddenly, I felt very close to.

Word of the incident quickly got around the NDP. The doctor was evacuated back to the rear, reports reached the command center that several men had made threats of killing him for refusing to leave the baseball game, and allowing the man to die.

I will never forget that day as long as I live. For me, it marked a change in the way I saw the war and the value of human life. It was a very long time before I could listen to the World Series again, and it has never brought about the excitement for me that it did as a kid.

The next day elements of the 2nd/2nd made their way into the battle area to help police up the dead and look for wounded. During our evening briefing on October 18th, we were told that as the VC left the battle they left behind a few soldiers to mop up what was left of the American battalion. They mutilated the bodies of many of the Americans. They cut heads off American soldiers and switched them around, putting black heads on white bodies and white heads on black bodies. At least one American soldier was found with over twenty AK47 rounds in his chest where his Combat Infantry Badge had been. After the briefing, our battalion commander issued the order that under no circumstance was an American soldier of the 2nd/2nd ever to be left behind for any reason. As far as I know, that order was never broken.

Later, what was left of the 2nd/28th Battalion was moved back to Lai Khe for an extended rest while the division brought in more men to rebuild the battalion. In the meantime, bodies had to be identified and letters had to be written.

CHAPTER 20

THANKSGIVING AND CHRISTMAS IN VIETNAM

Most of October and November were spent doing road security on Highway 13, Thunder Road, North of Lai Khe. There were several firebases set up along the highway, known as Thunder I through Thunder IV, and we furnished security for the firebases, swept Thunder Road every morning, and provided road security all along Highway 13 during the day.

Every day it was the same routine. I used the opportunity to do additional training on the radar for the new guys. We would set up the radar and monitor the traffic moving along the highway. We tracked everything including foot traffic, bicycles, ox carts, Jeeps, ¾-ton trucks, larger trucks, APCs, and tanks. This afforded the opportunity to learn the different sounds and patterns that each made. Some of the guys got so good they could tell the difference between a "duce and a half" and a 5-ton truck.

Nights were spent monitoring the open areas around the perimeters and the highway running through, or past the perimeter. It was during this time we got our first demonstration of flame fougasse. A fifty-five-gallon drum of napalm was set against a mound of dirt with an explosive charge attached to the barrel. When the charge was ignited, the napalm was blown for about fifty meters in an arch in front of the barrel and fire rained down on the jungle. It was surely what hell must look like. What a great defense against a ground attack, although I never saw it used except for that one demonstration.

A few days later I was instructed to move the Radar Teams up to Thunder IV, near Chon Thanh. We generally monitored activity in a large open area east of the perimeter. One day we had a Vietnamese barber come into the perimeter. He had his clippers, combs, money, etc. in a one-gallon can and was walking from position to position on the perimeter selling his services. It had been a while since I had seen a barber so I had him cut my hair. He cut a couple of the other guys and moved on to the next position. I started watching him and noticed that he would pull out a piece of paper and write something on it. We all started watching him and it became apparent that his selection of positions seemed to be more than just a random selection. I walked over to the TOC and told them what was going on. We had a detachment of Army of the Republic of Vietnam (ARVN) Military Police (QC) working with us, so, they were informed to check him out. He finished his rounds and as he was leaving, the QC detained him. When they emptied

Flame Fougasse, December 1967

his bucket, they found a detailed map of the perimeter with some of the more interesting positions clearly marked. We could hear the screaming and yelling as the interrogation got very heated. The QC beat the hell out of this guy to get as much info as possible out of him. Then they tied him up and put him in a Jeep and were gone. During our evening briefing I got a look at the map and was surprised at how accurate it was, and to find our radar position clearly marked. Although the radar was taken down and stored every morning he still determined that something about our position was interesting enough for him to mark us as a target.

Later that day, I developed a rash all over my back and chest. I went to the medics and they gave me some of that "magic" white cream to put on it. It was apparent that the rash was related to the haircut. I don't know if it was someone else's hair that was left on the clippers, or if it was the powder on his brush, but something from that haircut had given me that rash.

We celebrated Thanksgiving in the field at one of the Thunder bases. The mess sergeant managed to get a couple of whole turkeys and plenty of rolled turkeys. The whole turkeys were not enough for everyone but they looked nice sitting on the tables in the chow line as we were given our ample share of rolled turkey and dressing, along with all the trimmings "just like mom made." Almost, but not quite nearly!

HHC's Mess Sergeant was an old timer, and well connected. He was known to take a nip on a regular basis and on this trip out to the field the mess truck was thoroughly searched to make sure he didn't have any booze stashed in the equipment. Several bottles were taken off the truck before it was reloaded and sent on its way. On the second day in the field, some Special Forces officers arrived and went straight to the mess tent. One of the officers knew the mess sergeant from a previous assignment. They were looking for some American food. They were living with the ARVNs as advisors and were tired of eating rice and fish heads. "Cookie" wanted to know if they had anything to trade and the deal was on. They were shipped more booze than they could handle, and gladly traded enough to more than replace what was taken from him in Lai Khe for the Jeep load of food he gave them. He quickly hid his booze and once again Cookie was a happy man.

One day a general officer came for a visit. He and Cookie knew each other well. There was no saluting between them just a heartfelt handshake. On some days the evening meals were cooked in the mess hall in Lai Khe and flown in by chopper in thermal containers. When we did get new supplies of food they also came in by chopper. The general asked Cookie if he needed anything and the first thing out of his mouth was ice cream. "Sir, we haven't had ice cream in months." The general said he would see what he could do and the next day, right after the evening meal had been served, in came another chopper with bunches of ice cream. It was just loaded on the chopper in boxes with nothing to keep it cold so it was pretty much melted by the time it got there. A few guys came back to the mess tent to get some but word got out that it was mostly melted so most didn't bother to walk back to get any. The ground surveillance sleeping area was set up close to the mess tent so every night for a week we were given a half gallon of ice cream apiece and tried to eat it before it had completely melted. What a mess but it was wonderful! After a week, the ice cream chopper no longer came but we enjoyed it while it lasted.

While we were in Thunder IV, the commo (communications) group got a new technician who knew how to work on the radar units. He managed to get another unit running for us so we could set up two positions on the perimeter. Since we were planning to be in this location for a while they started running commo wire so we could use telephones in the perimeter. The guys from commo were busting their asses to get the wires run, set up a switchboard, and distribute phones to certain locations. One evening the new tech came over and asked if I would please call his platoon leader and request that he be sent over to work on the radar. Setting up those field phones was kicking his ass. So, I waited for him to get back to laying wire and made the call. The lieutenant really didn't want to let him go but finally relented and sent him over. The tech came over, opened a radar unit, and lit up some weed. After he had been there about fifteen minutes the lieutenant called to see what he was doing. He told the lieutenant that the "butterfly oscillator" that controlled the "beam deflector" had a problem but he almost had it fixed. The lieutenant bought it and gave him fifteen minutes more to get it fixed or send it back to the rear and let them handle it. He finished his joint and went back to stringing wire. That was the last time I offered to do him a favor.

Towards the end of November, we started receiving our Christmas CARE packages from home. Charlie Matthews' wife sent him a three-foot aluminum Christmas tree, complete with silver and red glass balls, and an Angel for the top. Although some of the balls were broken during the trip over, most of them were in good shape. We put the tree on a table in the corner of the barracks and attached our Christmas cards to it. It was almost like being at home. We bought some Christmas lights in the village but every time we plugged them in a light burned out. Since we couldn't get replacement bulbs, and the rest of the lights wouldn't work if one light was burned out, I started cutting the bulbs out and twisting the wire together. This, of course, made the lights glow a little brighter each time I cut one out, but it also made them burn out faster. The string of lights didn't last long. To improvise, we put red lenses in our flashlights and put them under and around the tree to light it up.

In early December the battalion moved back into Lai Khe, after spending Thanksgiving in the field. We were hoping to stay there through Christmas, and maybe even get a chance to see Bob Hope when he came to Lai Khe. But as luck would have it, after only a few days in Lai Khe, we got orders to move out.

We moved north of Lai Khe and set up a perimeter just outside the Hoi Chanh village. There was an ARVN base camp about fifty meters south of the village and we were camped about two hundred meters south of them, on the crest of a

Christmas tree in Lai Khe, 1967

small hill. Every evening just before nightfall our interpreter, Tham, would go into the ARVN base camp and spend the night. After it got dark we would set up the radar and point it in the direction of the ARVN base camp and the village. We monitored the activity around the base camp and the village as well as the open areas surrounding the village. Between 10:00 and 11:00 P.M., every night, we would detect movement leaving the village and going into the ARVN base camp. Then around 1:00 to 2:00 A.M. we would detect the movement going from the base camp, back into the village. We never told Tham that we were monitoring the base camp with the radar, but we did ask him about the movement that took place every night. At first, he was confused as to how we knew so much about what was going on, but he finally confessed that the ARVNs were bringing women out of the village. They were smoking dope, drinking beer and rice wine, and partying with the girls. We were supposed to be depending on these guys to watch our flank and they were getting stoned and having sex.

After about a week, we moved back into Lai Khe. We knew for sure we were going to get to stay in for Christmas now. It was getting too close to the holiday for the division to be mounting another exercise. Hell, even wars need to have some time off to enjoy the holidays. Wrong!

On December 22, a sapper infiltrated the ammo dump at Lai Khe and set off several charges. The 2nd/2nd was ordered to bring in the APCs and search the ammo dump for the dead and wounded. Our guys went into the dump while the rounds were still exploding and placed the APCs in harm's way while they searched for dead and wounded. It was one hell of a deadly fireworks show. Although they managed to keep most of the fire and explosions out of the heavy artillery rounds, the ammo that was going off was sending slugs and brass in all directions.

The next morning, we were given orders to move out to the south. We were going to pull "Palace Guard" around the huge American installation of Long Binh. Our primary objective was to secure the area for the *Bob Hope Show* and we would be there through Christmas and New Year's Eve.

Once we were dug in, we had a drawing to select a few lucky men to go back to Lai Khe for the *Bob Hope Show*. Bob Warren was selected to go from our group. We tried to buy his ticket from him but he wanted to get back to the barracks, take a long shower, eat some hot food, sleep in a comfortable bed, and write some letters, so he wouldn't sell that ticket for any price. The rest of us had to settle for listening to the show on the radio and using our imagination when we heard Joey Heatherton talking to Bob Hope. We all envied Warren for getting to be there for the show; that is until he returned to the field and told how they were treated.

When the lucky winners got back to Lai Khe, they were not allowed to go to their barracks. They were kept close to

Lai Khe ammo dump explosion,
December 22, 1967

the area where the show was being held, they had to sleep on the ground, eat C rations, and they weren't allowed to take a shower. Their seats for the show were all the way in the back of the audience and they could barely see the stage. As soon as the show was over, they were loaded into trucks in a resupply convoy and brought back to the field.

During the last week of December, one of our patrols ran into a small group of North Vietnamese soldiers. The NVA troops returned fire but immediately started moving away from the fight. One man was left behind to act as a sniper and slow the pursuit of the evading North Vietnamese. The battalion commander called for gunship support and we were treated to a demonstration of the Cobra Gunship, one of the newest weapons in the American arsenal. By the time the Cobras got on station, the NVA had disappeared into a thick area of jungle. The Cobras worked the area over with what they had on board and then offered to return to Long Binh, take on a full load, and come back for a full demonstration of their firepower. When the Cobras came back we were perched on the side of a hill and had a bird's eye view for the show. It was awesome! The gunships took turns making passes over the thicket. The machine guns, 40MM cannons, and 2.75-inch rockets were pouring into the jungle. It was hard to believe how much devastation could be put out by just one of these birds. It made me glad for two things. They were on my side, and I was getting very short. I only had a few weeks left in country.

The sniper who was left behind by the NVA was wounded and in an attempt to hide had crawled into the center of a thorny vine, commonly referred to by Americans as a "wait-a-minute vine." Attempts to get him out were futile as he continued to fight with all he had. He had to be killed and then pulled out of the vine for searching. They found papers on his body that indicated he was part of an NVA training organization. Their orders were to avoid all contact with enemy troops and concentrate on training activities.

A holiday "cease fire" was called, and we got to spend New Year's Eve in the field outside of Long Binh. A couple of days before New Year's Eve, four of us took a Jeep and trailer into Long Binh and loaded up on supplies for the occasion. I had a long list of booze orders from all over the battalion. I had orders from officers, Non-Coms, and enlisted men. We brought back a trailer full of booze and snacks (mostly booze).

While we were in Long Binh, one of the REMFs (Rear Echelon Mother Fuckers) came up to the Jeep and told me that I should take better care of my weapon. "If you need to use that in a firefight," he said, "it will probably jam because of all the dirt on it." I offered to show him how well it would work if he didn't get the hell away from me, and he left.

VC flag found hanging on bush outside Long Bien,
December 31, 1967

On the way back to the night defensive perimeter, I spotted a small Viet Cong flag hanging on a bush about twenty-five yards down a small side road. I stopped the Jeep and walked down the road to get the flag, never thinking that this might be a trap, or that the flag might be booby-trapped. Lucky for me, neither was the case. I carefully looked it over and removed it from the tree. When we got back to the NDP I took the flag to the Battalion Intelligence Officer to report it. He brushed it off by saying kids had probably made it out of construction paper as a joke and hung it out to see who would stop and pick it up.

Within a few weeks, the Tet Offensive of 1968 started. It turned out that the flag was put there to guide North Vietnamese and Viet Cong troops into staging areas. So much for Army Intelligence!

CHAPTER 21

THE BATTLE OF XOM BUNG – MY LAST OUTING

After pulling our time on "Palace Guard" the 2nd/2nd moved back to Lai Khe for a short rest. We stayed in Lai Khe for a few days and then moved southeast of Lai Khe and into the vicinity of the Crooked Village. This had long been a stronghold for the V.C. Phu Loi Battalion. When we moved in they sniped at us long enough to get us jumpy and ready for a fight and then they ran off into the jungle leaving the locals to deal with us. It was all very frustrating. As soon as we broke camp and moved out the VC were moving back in. The locals were very sympathetic to the VC cause, so we had to be on our best behavior while we were in this area. Deep down we all wanted to level the village but the word had come down that Congress had identified this as a "no fire zone." I saw one congressman fly over in a helicopter on one occasion the whole time I was in Vietnam. What the hell did they know about the war and how would they like being shot at and not being able to fire back? On this occasion, the rules got changed in an instant and Congress didn't get consulted.

All the units in the area were seeing contact, almost daily. On one occasion the 2nd/18th made contact with the VC Phu Loi Battalion near the village of Xom Bung. The 2nd/2nd was called in to help the 2nd/18th. After breaking contact with the VC both units moved back into their NDPs and called artillery and air strikes into the area. The pounding went on throughout the night resulting in over one hundred VC bodies being found the next day. Every man in the unit was on edge. Although the contacts were generally short, they were more frequent than we had ever seen.

One night while I was manning the radar unit I picked up movement about 150 to 200 meters from the perimeter. I was positive this was people moving down a road. I could hear what I thought were the wheels of a cart, along with the movements of several people and/or large animals. When I reported the sighting to TOC the OD called in mortars on the area. That was followed by artillery and then by heavy fire support from Naval guns. The forward observer (FO) called me and instructed me to adjust fire. Once the heavy rounds started landing they seemed to be right on top of us. I told the FO that they were too damn close, "Back them up! Back them up!" He pulled the guns back 50 to 100 meters and started working them down the road and around the area.

When the artillery finished, a mounted APC patrol was sent into the area. They picked up movement and started

Ground Surveillance Team and APC standing guard around TOC

firing on it. About ten minutes into the firefight we saw the huts burst into flames. The fight was over and it was quiet for the remainder of the night.

First thing the next morning we got orders to pack up and move back to Lai Khe. Before leaving the area, several helicopters with generals from Division Headquarters dropped in for a talk. The ground surveillance section was ordered to position ourselves into a small perimeter around the TOC until the generals left. By the time they finished their visit most of the Battalion was on its way back to Lai Khe. The generals got back into their helicopters, flew over the burned-out huts and disappeared into the sky. I guessed someone had to explain to Congress just what had happened in their "No Fire Zone."

We arrived in Lai Khe with me having less than two weeks left in country. I was convinced that my war was over and, from here on out, I could spend my time packing, buying trinkets for my wife and family, and trying to wash off the new layer of laterite dust I had accumulated since R&R. I was almost right.

CHAPTER 22

PREPARING TO LEAVE

Most of the unit stood down for a week while one company was out running road security. After a week of being back in the Lai Khe base camp, I was convinced that I was too short to go back to the field. Then the order came down to pack up and move out. The unit was going north to position ourselves somewhere between An Loc and Loc Ninh. The war had been getting really heavy, especially around Loc Ninh. The 25th Division was getting their ass kicked badly in Loc Ninh, and the Big Red One was going up there to even out the fight. I got to thinking about how close I was to going home, and the stories I had read about men being killed with only a few days left, and I decided I wanted no part of this fight. I talked it over with Charlie Mathews and Bob Warren and decided I was going to the section leader and request that we not go. The request was denied on the spot so I told him that he had better start the courts martial proceeding on me because I felt I had done my part and was not going to go. I knew if push came to shove I would pack my shit and get in the Jeep but I wanted to be the one doing the pushing for a change. He looked at me for a while and finally said he would talk to the company commander about me staying behind. I told him that he had to talk to CPT Green about Charlie and Bob as well. He left and about 15 minutes later came back and said CPT Green had granted permission for me and Charlie to stay behind but Bob had to go because his DEROS (date expected to return from overseas) was a couple of days later than Charlie's and mine. Bob loaded his gear and got on the truck. They moved somewhere north of An Loc and set up a staging area for resupply before the unit moved further north. Bob spent one night in the field and the next morning he was on a chopper back to Lai Khe.

Charlie and I were placed on Charge of Quarters (CQ) duty in the company area while we were waiting to clear. We took turns manning the orderly room on alternating nights for our remaining time in Lai Khe. Charlie and I had both managed to pick up .45 semi-automatic pistols that we were planning to take home. Charlie took his apart and put it inside his tape recorder. He had to take out most of the circuit boards to make it fit but he left enough electronics in it to make the reels turn. It looked good but it sure was heavy. I took my pistol apart and put parts of it in a bottle of talcum powder. I slit the lining on my AWOL bag and carefully taped the big pieces to the side of the bag under the lining. I then taped cardboard over the pistol so it couldn't be felt from inside the bag. I had several people look at it and tell me what they thought and none of them could find the pistol. It looked like I was going to get home with a real souvenir from the war.

I spent my nights on CQ duty writing poems about being short and going home, or letters to the people back home that I planned to deliver personally. Then one night the silence was broken by incoming rounds. Mortar rounds and rockets were exploding all over the company area. I grabbed my letters and poems and ran for a hole. The bombardment only lasted a few minutes but it was enough to keep me on my toes for the rest of the night. After the all-clear was sounded I didn't feel easy sitting in the orderly room with the lights on so I shut them off and watched out through the screen that surrounded the building. This was my last night in Lai Khe and I wasn't going to take any chances.

When morning came I went to the barracks to pack the few things I wanted to take back with me. I managed to get what I

A mortar round hit a tree in front of the barracks, January 1968—
my last night in Lai Khe

wanted in a single AWOL bag and donated the rest of the stuff
to those who were staying behind. A mortar round had hit a
rubber tree just outside the barracks. The round exploded
in the top of the tree and rained shell fragments through the
tin roof of the barracks. I found a piece of the mortar round
buried in the floor under my bunk. I couldn't help but wonder
if I hadn't been on CQ Duty, would I have been in the bunk
when it passed through the mattress? I dug it out of the floor
and threw it in my AWOL bag along with a fragment from a
120mm rocket that had buried itself in the ground just outside the barracks next to ours. Then Charlie and I were off to
Di An to clear division.

When we got to division I was concerned about the inspection that my AWOL bag would be given. As we stood in
formation waiting to process out, an officer asked if we had
anything that we wanted to leave in country. He said he would
turn his back and if any illegal arms or ammunition fell on the
ground he would not ask where it came from. If they found it
later we would be prosecuted and spend time at Long Binh
Jail. The week before we got there some soldier took an 81MM

mortar round out of his duffel bag and threw it in front of the formation. I elected to take my chances and much to my surprise the inspection was waived. The officer told us our belongings would be checked very thoroughly at Long Binh so we had one more chance to get rid of anything we shouldn't be taking home.

As we went through the final paperwork clearance, Charlie was told that he was going to have to stay one day longer than I was. I had come in country on February 2nd and he came in on February 3rd. He was still allowed to go to Long Binh with me but he wasn't booked on a flight until the morning after I left Vietnam.

We boarded a helicopter and we were off to Long Binh. When we got to the Out-Processing Center we checked in and got ourselves a bunk. We were to go through Out-Processing and Baggage Inspection the following afternoon. I decided to see what kind of inspection they were giving the bags so I went to the Out-Processing area to watch.

Each man was assigned to a small table. He was instructed to unpack all his bags and put the contents on the table and the bags under the table. The inspectors made a very thorough examination of the goods on the tables. Once they had unfolded and thrown around what was on the table, they picked up the bags, turned them upside down, and shook them. They folded and rolled the empty duffle bags and then threw them on the table. After they looked at all the stuff on the tables, some twice, they instructed everyone to repack their shit and get on the bus.

I went back to the barracks and told Charlie what I had just watched. I was afraid the tape holding the gun inside my AWOL bag would let go when they shook it, and I decided to get rid of the gun. The next morning, I found some troops who were just coming in country and asked them if they wanted to buy a .45-caliber pistol for $25. One guy jumped right on the deal and we went to the barracks to make the exchange. I pulled the lining out, ripped the gun parts out, and gave them to him. I gave him the bottle of talcum powder with the small parts in it and he gave me $25. After we made the exchange I asked him what he was going to be doing in Vietnam. That is when he scared the living shit out of me. He told me that he was an MP and was getting assigned to the MP detachment at Long Binh. He said he was glad he got the gun because he wanted to carry a spare and he knew they would not issue him two pistols. We parted ways and I went to the PX to spend my new cash.

Charlie and I said our goodbyes and made plans to meet in California. We talked about staying in San Francisco for a couple of days to see what those "flower children" were really like. We both knew that once we got back to the States it was going to be nonstop until we got back to our wives and our folks. Around 3:00 P.M. I went to the Out-Processing area to get inspected. I laid all my stuff on the table and put my AWOL bag under the table. The Inspector came by and said, "Is this all you're taking home? Traveling light, aren't you?" He then kicked my AWOL bag and told me to pack up. I convinced myself right then that I would have gotten caught either at the Tan Son Nhut airport or when we went through Customs in California. There was no inspection at Tan Son Nhut, and the Customs guy in California had me open my bag and he picked up one pair of underwear and told me to go on through.

As we passed through the Out-Processing building I couldn't help but remember going through this building twelve months earlier on the other side of the tables. There were some green troops coming in and we shouted the same things at them that pissed me off when I came in country. Looking back now, it didn't seem like it had been a year. But I was still not willing to stay one minute longer than I had to.

We boarded the 707 at 5:00 P.M. We were the last flight out for the day. As it turned out, we were the last flight out before the Tet Offensive of 1968 slowed things down considerably. Shortly after we left, the airport and surrounding support facilities started getting incoming mortar and rocket fire. Charlie was flown to the Philippines after a couple of days and had to wait there a week before he could fly home. The news of the Tet Offensive reached home before I did and people were really concerned about the turn the war had just taken. I had been home a couple of days before I sat down and watched the news. I told everyone that the VC knew better than to start that shit while I was still in country. At the same time, I was counting my blessings that I got out of there before it all started.

The official reports show that the Tet Offensive started on January 31, 1968, at 3:00 A.M. It started much earlier than that. As early as October 1967, we were seeing signs of a massive troop buildup in the 1st Infantry Division area of operations. The ass kicking the 2nd/28th took in October was from a force, which according to Army Intelligence, wasn't even in the area. There were lots of reports of small firefights where American troops stumbled upon NVA and/or VC troops and started a firefight. The main force of the enemy very quickly broke off the engagements and ran away leaving only one or two snipers behind to slow pursuit by American troops. They were saving their strength for the Tet Offensive. The NVA troops we ran into around Christmas '67 were a training group that was in the area to coordinate the battle. The VC flag I took off the tree outside Long Binh was there to mark the way to NVA and VC staging areas. It is all very clear now, but at the time no one could put all the pieces of the puzzle together.

CHAPTER 23

THE FREEDOM BIRD

What a great feeling it was to get on that "Freedom Bird" and head back to the "World"—home, a place I wasn't sure I would ever see again, to be around the people I loved and missed. Shortly after liftoff the pilot came on the PA system and told us that an American ship, the USS *Pueblo*, had been captured by the North Koreans and he had received orders to divert the flight to South Korea so we could be pressed into service there. He very quickly made it clear that he was joking and welcomed us aboard and thanked us for our service in Vietnam. We made a brief stop in Okinawa and then on to Travis Air Force Base in California. A quick trip through Customs and we were on a bus to Oakland Army Terminal for new winter uniforms, a steak dinner, processing, and duty station orders, and then on to San Francisco to fly home. Five of us grabbed a taxi at Oakland and headed for the airport in San Francisco. We were on the driver's ass to drive as fast as he could so we could catch our flights. The driver tried his best to get us to the airport on time and the guys were handing me money to pay and tip him for his efforts. I don't know how much money I had in my hands, but when I handed it to the driver he offered to carry all our bags in for us.

I tried to buy a full-fare ticket to Indianapolis but the agent refused and said he would only sell me a stand-by ticket. I told him cost was no object and I sure as hell didn't want to miss my flight home. He told me not to worry because he would take care of me. There were three of us, Wayne Brady, a Marine, and me on the same flight and we ran through the airport to get to the gate. Just as we arrived at the gate, they were taking three people off the full flight so we could get on. The folks who had been taken off were not happy, but we were and didn't mind the glares we got from them as we boarded the flight. I was seated by an older woman who owned a bar near the Naval Station in San Diego and made her living selling drinks to sailors. She evidently had a few before she left the bar because she talked and flirted until she finally fell asleep. She was heading to Chicago, our first stop, to go to her dad's funeral. We arrived in Chicago and I parted ways with Wayne. He lived near Chicago and I was catching a plane to Indianapolis along with the Marine who was also returning from Vietnam. He had been charged full fare for his ticket. We were just about the only passengers on the flight from Chicago to Indianapolis. Shortly after leaving the ground the stewardess came by and asked to see my ticket. After seeing that it was a stand by ticket she asked me if I would like to move into first class. I jumped at the chance to spend the next hour or so sitting in luxury. So much better than sitting in a Jeep or in the sling seats of a Huey. I asked if they were going to bring the Marine up and she said she wasn't allowed to because he had paid full fare for his ticket. That ticket agent in San Francisco was still taking care of me! I was the only passenger in first class and had two stewardesses taking care of me. About thirty minutes after I had moved up, there was a loud squeal in the cabin. The pilot came back to check it out and told me they had lost a seal on the boarding door and I would have to move back to Coach Class. I took my AWOL bag and moved as far away from the squealing door as I could get.

We arrived in Indianapolis around 6 A.M. I gathered my belongings and called my wife so she could come to pick me up. That is the first time I heard anything about the Tet Offensive. No one knew I was coming home and they all thought I was still there, caught up in that mess. It took her about an hour to get dressed and make it to the airport. I walked outside and sat on the curb waiting for her. An old colored man, one of the porters at the airport, came up to me and asked if I was OK. I said, "yes, sir, I am doing fine." He asked if I had just got back from Vietnam and I said, "Yes, sir, I did." He then said, "Well son, let me be the first one to welcome you home." It would be many years before I heard that phrase from a total stranger again.

I had been sending most of my pay home from Vietnam and my wife had bought us a new 1968 Mustang just before I got home. I let her drive us back to the apartment because I wasn't sure I could find my way around Indianapolis right now. Around noon we went to her parents' home where part of her family had gathered to welcome me home. Later that afternoon we drove to my uncle's house where some friends had gathered for dinner. I'm not sure what I expected but I certainly didn't feel like I was given that typical "Welcome Home" party you see on TV or in the movies. It was almost like they were more interested in talking to each other than they were in the returning hero! I certainly didn't consider myself a hero, but I just expected a little more interest from folks about where I had been and what I had been doing for the past year. I had no idea what sort of stigma being a Vietnam Vet carried with it!

We stayed in Indianapolis for a couple of weeks before heading to my parents' house in New Mexico. I finally got behind the wheel of that Mustang and drove it just like I had driven that Jeep during convoys in Vietnam, ten miles per hour through the city and fifteen miles per hour in the open spaces. My wife and sister-in-law were in the car one day and we were driving down Michigan Street. I thought I was busting it at twenty miles per hour but was being honked at and passed on both sides by the other cars. Joyce was laughing her ass off in the back seat because I was driving so slowly. That is when I decided I was going to have to bite the bullet and push that accelerator a little harder if I was going to survive civilian traffic again.

We packed all our worldly possessions in the trunk and back seat of that Mustang and headed for New Mexico. We drove straight through, stopping only for gas, food, and potty breaks. I did manage to get that Mustang well over eighty miles per hour during the trip and felt I had learned to drive once more. Before going into the Army, I had several speeding tickets and was about to lose my license. During Basic Training, I got a letter from a judge in Indiana ordering me to report to his courtroom and explain why I shouldn't lose my license. I gave it to the company commander and he wrote a letter to the judge explaining why he wouldn't be seeing me in his courtroom. I was given twelve months' probation. Any violation would result in my license being revoked. It had been well over a year and I was back to my old habits again.

We arrived at my parents' home in the wee hours of the morning. My wife asked how we were going to get in the house. I told her, "This is Monument, New Mexico. We will just walk in the front door." She was amazed when I walked up, opened the front door, and walked into the house. We had brought in our suitcases before I walked back to my parents' bedroom and woke them up. We sat in the front room talking for a while and dad said, "Well, hell, it's time to get up, let's put the coffee on."

I said, "Well, hell, it's time to get some sleep. Show me to a bed." Mom went to their bedroom and put new sheets on the bed and told us to go in there. It would be much quieter than the other bedrooms. We went to bed and slept until late afternoon.

It was great being with my family once again, but the reception was about the same as I got in Indianapolis. I just couldn't figure out what was going on. I expected more questions and way more hugs. I had no idea of the stigma that had been cast on the American fighting man by the news media. Most of it untrue, but never let the truth stand in the way of a good story.

CHAPTER 24

FORT HOOD, TEXAS – RIOT CONTROL TRAINING

After two weeks in New Mexico, we headed for Fort Hood, Texas. That was to be our home for the next six months unless a slick reenlistment NCO could talk me into signing up again. We arrived in Killeen, Texas and found a motel to stay in until we could get base housing or an apartment. I was assigned to the 2nd Battalion, 52nd Infantry Regiment, 1st Armor Division. I had never heard of an Infantry Regiment in an Armor Division. In Vietnam, the armor units were assigned to infantry divisions and sent to support the infantry battalions. We drove to the base the night before I was to report so I could locate my unit. After driving around the base for a while, I saw lights on in a building and stopped to see if I could get some help. I walked in and waited for someone to come from the back room and help me. When the guy walked out my jaw hit the floor. The guy said, "Man, you look like you just saw a dead man." It was one of the guys I had gotten to know who worked with the C Company Commander. CPT Rose was a fantastic Commander and I especially enjoyed it when we got attached to C Company because I knew we were going to be treated as part of the family. And the mess sergeant in C Company was the best in the battalion so we knew we were going to eat good as well. It was a very sad day when CPT

Rose's command APC hit a mine and everyone on the APC was reported as KIA, including the guy who was standing in front of me. We chatted for a while, and he told me he was wounded pretty bad and unconscious when he was medevacked out. He was shipped to Japan for a while and then back to the states for a full recovery.

The next day I reported to my new assignment. I was assigned to ground surveillance as second in charge. SGT Bedell was a career soldier who had spent some time in Germany and married a German girl before being shipped back to the States. So far, he had managed to avoid Vietnam but his luck was about to run out at any time. He was having problems with his wife because she didn't want him to go to Vietnam and leave her in America where she didn't know anyone. He didn't have the money to send her and their kid back to Germany so he was working evenings at a Quick Shop store off base every chance he could. That wasn't helping the marriage either. His regular second in charge was locked up in jail on drug charges awaiting his day in court. The rest of the section was made up of misfits that no one else wanted so Bedell took them to get in good with the SGT Major. They were drinking buddies and that wasn't helping his marriage either. To top it off, the section didn't even have a single radar unit. Our days went something like this. Morning chow, followed by police call, then down to the motor pool to pull maintenance on Jeeps that we weren't allowed to take out of the motor pool. We would drive them around the large fenced area and wash them. Then do whatever preventive maintenance was required. Then we would go to the empty equipment room and do "beautification" on and around it. That meant putting a fresh coat of paint on things that didn't need to be painted, including the rocks that lined the sidewalk leading up to the door of the building.

When we broke for noon chow, most of them went to the mess hall, but since I had off-base housing I would be required to pay to eat in the chow hall. So, I drove home where my wife had lunch fixed. We ate lunch and watched most of a soap opera before I headed back to the base. There was a formation after lunch, mostly to count heads, and then we were released for training. We didn't have any radar units so what were we supposed to train on? We walked to the motor pool, unlocked our little building and hung out for a while. Once the "powers that be" had driven by and saw we were in there looking busy, we were free to sneak off for some free time, but could not leave the base. SGT Bedell gave me a notebook and a pen to carry in my shirt pocket. We grabbed a private and headed for the PX. We would all go in and order a cold drink and sit there and shoot the breeze or play the pinball machines. If an officer walked in we would jump to our feet and start chewing out the private for leaving the area without permission. Pull out the notebook and pen and tell him we were putting him on notice. Then grab him by the arm and leave. I am sure the officers knew what we were doing, but, if it looked good they let it slide.

About once a month I had to pull CQ duty at battalion headquarters. There would be an LT, acting as Officer of the Day, an SPC 4, the OD's driver, and me, the non-commissioned officer in charge (NCOIC). The OD and his driver were allowed to sleep during the night if they made regular patrols. The NCOIC had to be awake always. I soon learned to lie on the double seat that set next to the front door with my feet sticking over the armrest and in front of the door. If anyone tried to come in the door they would hit my feet with the door and I would be sitting up by the time they made it into the orderly room. Although that didn't happen very often, it was a benefit to catch a few minutes of sleep every now and then.

A couple of times a night I would take turns with the OD to go out and check the guards. About the only thing we guarded were the warehouses, especially the medical supply warehouse. Drug use was rampant in the late '60s and that warehouse had been broken into several times to get drugs.

One of the LTs that I usually pulled CQ with was fresh out of OCS and this was his first duty station. Because of my experience in Vietnam, he pretty much considered us to be equal. He loved to play board games that had to do with war. He had started that in OCS and was pretty good at it. He said it helped him build his strategic thinking. One evening we were playing The Battle of the Bulge. I don't remember that much about the game but it had to do with rolling dice and drawing cards off the deck with instruction and then making your move. It was a very long game, not meant to be finished in one sitting, so we had played it several times. In one part of the game the allies were trying to resupply the main force troops and they only had a certain number of days to get it done before they ran out of ammo and lost to the Germans. I was playing the part of the Germans. I decided to use the same tactics the NVA and VC were using on us just before the Tet offensive. I would leave small forces of men behind to slow down the convoy and move my main force ahead. It started to work and by the time we had finished the evening's game I had defeated the allied forces, something that did not happen during the actual war. The LT was flabbergasted because he had played this game several times in OCS and never lost. Maybe it taught him a little different slant on warfare.

I had CQ duty on July 4th. We were sitting around the desk playing the board game. I had my back to the open window, the LT was across from me, and the driver was sitting at the end of the desk. I was deep in thought planning my next move when someone lit a string of firecrackers right outside the window. In a flash, I was on the floor under the desk while the LT and the driver were laughing their asses off. I told them that wouldn't be so funny once they had a chance to spend some time in Vietnam and the laughing stopped. A few weeks later LT got his orders for Vietnam and came looking for me with lots of questions about what he could expect when he got in country.

Dr. Martin Luther King was assassinated in the evening on Thursday, April 4, 1968. Within a couple of hours, rioting had started in several major cities across the US. I had a three-day weekend pass coming up the next day for my birthday on April 6th. I reported to the orderly room very early on the morning on the 5th to sign out and get on the road to New Mexico because I had a feeling that something was going to happen and we were going to be involved. I told my wife to leave the car radio turned off until we got to my parents' house. I did not want to hear anything about all leaves and passes being canceled. If I didn't hear it, it didn't happen. I don't know if it happened or not, although my unit was called Friday morning to report for riot control duty in Chicago. They went to Chicago and spent the week in Jackson Park on the South side of Chicago.

When I returned on Monday, the First Sergeant (TOP) was pissed that I had managed to miss making the trip with the rest of the unit. He chewed my ass out and told me to go home and pack a duffle bag and report back to him within the hour. He was going to get my ass shipped to Chicago to be with my unit. I think he was mostly pissed because I hadn't done anything wrong and had managed to outsmart the Army.

For the rest of the day, I was sent from one unit to the other to see if I could get a ride to Chicago. When that didn't work I was put on 24-hour CQ duty. I had 24 hours on and 24 hours off. Killeen was a ghost town when it came to men. Some units were shipped to Austin, Texas to catch rides on Air Force planes to Chicago, and most of them spent the week sitting on the runways because the planes never left. This exercise was a total mess. No one had ever trained for riot control duty and that was about to change.

When the units came back from Chicago and Austin, training for riot control was started. During the day we had step jab training. Bayonets were fixed to empty rifles, we were put on line, with the officers and a sniper behind us, and we did this step jab movement designed to move angry mobs to the rear. Take a step forward, stop and jab the rifle with a bayonet attached towards the crowd with a loud holler. We spent days practicing that maneuver.

Then came the early morning calls that we were being scrambled to fly someplace to control crowds. The first time I was called at 2:00 A.M. and told to report to my unit ready to be sent out of town for up to a week. The duffle bag was already packed and in the car so I got to base as quickly as I could. On one of these calls, I got a speeding ticket soon after getting on base. For an E-5 that was an automatic bust to an SPC 4 or Corporal. I did manage to get out of it when a guy I took basic training with saw my name come across the "blotter" for speeding. He managed to erase it and get rid of the ticket. A return favor for a huge favor I had done for him during a forced night march at Fort Knox, Kentucky over eighteen months ago. On this night I got to my unit and we were put on trucks to be taken to the awaiting airplanes at the Ft. Hood airport.

After sitting on the trucks for an hour we were taken off the trucks and sat on the ground for half an hour and loaded back on the trucks. We were finally released for breakfast and told to report back to the trucks after we ate. We were screwed with the whole day and not allowed to return to the barracks. Finally, at 2:00 A.M. the following morning we were put on the trucks and taken to the airport. We made it onto the planes, took a seat for about thirty minutes and were told to deplane and return to the trucks. Driven back to the company area and released with orders to report for regular duty the next morning.

The next exercise was to perform actual riot control on the base. The 2nd Armor Division was to play the part of rioters and the 1st Armor Division was to perform riot control duty. My unit was shipped out into the country and set up two-man tents to live in for the next three days. We were the reserve unit for controlling the rioters. They had been nice enough to mow a huge field for us to camp in. The field was full of poison oak, poison ivy, and chiggers. We sat there for three days and never left the area.

When it came time for us to return to the main fort after the riots had stopped, trucks came to pick us up. The company commander decided that we didn't need those trucks and we were going to march back to the company area. After all, it was only ten miles or so. He did march part of the way with us then got in his Jeep and left. Just as we came within a few blocks of the company area he was back and took up his position at the head of the formation and proudly marched back into the company area with us. As we passed by the parking lots we saw that most of the cars were covered with white powder. The rioters had been throwing bags of flour to make the riot look more realistic. Water was used to control the crowds and what was left on the cars didn't come off without damaging the paint. The whole exercise was one big screw-up but according to the company commander, "Much valuable information was learned by the cadre."

Shortly after that exercise, I was called into the Reenlistment NCO's office for a very short talk. He started out by telling me how great the Army was and what they would do for me if I gave them another six years. I told him I wasn't interested and his attitude changed. He said, "I bet you have a great job waiting for you when you get out and the pay is way better than what the Army can give you." I told him that the job wasn't that fantastic but they never ask me to go camp out in a field loaded with poison oak, poison ivy, and chiggers for three days and then force march me back to town. I was promptly kicked out of his office!

We had some great friends at Fort Hood. No one had any money so we often just sat around, played cards and board games, and enjoyed each other's company. One night we were all sitting around my apartment and decided to treat ourselves with a trip to Dairy Queen. It was almost the end of the month so we were pretty much living on pocket change. We decided to "march" to the Dairy Queen to save gas. The ladies freshened up their makeup and fixed their hair, after all we were going out in public, and off we went. Jim and I started taking turns calling cadence as we got the ladies into step and marched down the street. We found lots of things to do that required very little if no money and had a great time. Sometimes I look back on those years and think they were among the best years of my adult life.

I started processing out of the Army a couple of days before my expiration of term of service (ETS). On the evening before my last day, riots broke out in Chicago during the Democratic National Convention. Once again, the units at Fort Hood were put on alert for riot control duty. The day I got out of the Army my unit was being shipped to Chicago. I dodged that bullet again! And once again TOP was pissed at me because there was nothing he could do about me not making the trip with them.

CHAPTER 25

LIFE AFTER THE ARMY

After my separation from the Army, we drove back to Indianapolis where we stayed with relatives until we could find an apartment. We had managed to acquire more household goods than what would fit in the Mustang, and since I was an E-5, the Army moved our stuff for us. We had a little less than thirty days to find a place to put our stuff, or it would have to be put into storage. We found a two-bedroom apartment on the west side of Indianapolis, near where I would go back to work for RCA. We went shopping for furniture and all the other things a young couple would need to set up housekeeping.

Within a week I was back at my old job at RCA. On the first day I pulled some parts, laid out the blueprint, laid out my inspection tools, and for the life of me, I could not remember how to use them. It was one of those moments that made me wonder if I should have stayed in the Army where my skill-set was still sharp. I struggled with those thoughts often over the next few years. I remember thinking that my job had no meaning and my life had no mission. I was building TV sets for God's sake. Who really needed a new TV set? Although I was not an alcoholic, I did like drinking booze on the weekends. A party was nothing unless I got hammered.

A little over a year later our first daughter was born. Once again life started to have a mission. There were all those dirty diapers to change and all those late-night feedings. For the first time in a while, I had plenty to keep my mind busy. But that wouldn't last forever. The weekend boozing slowed way down and we were spending less time with friends who didn't have kids. I worked the day shift and my wife worked the night shift so I had daddy duties in the evenings and all night. One evening I was having a hard time with my daughter. She didn't want to go to sleep and it was getting very late. After what seemed like an eternity of trying to get her to sleep, I lost my cool and threw her bottle against the wall, splattering milk all over the room and on her. She stopped crying and just looked at me, with milk splashed on her face. I told myself how stupid that was and began to clean up the mess. While I was working on it, my daughter finally went to sleep. I went into the front room and sat in a corner and cried uncontrollably. This was my first outburst caused by post-traumatic stress disorder (PTSD), but I had no idea what was happening. When my wife got home, she was pissed that she found me that way and told me to straighten up! Tough love!

My career had plenty of ups and downs. Thankfully, there were more ups than downs. I managed to move up the ladder at RCA and finally got myself into college. The local university offered an exploratory path that would allow me to take up to twenty-five credit hours without selecting a major and without going through the registration process. That was a blessing because if they saw my high school transcript, they probably wouldn't let me take classes.

I found a counselor I really liked and registered for one of his classes. I liked that class so well I took another and then another. Before long I was hooked into the Supervision Program at IUPUI (Indiana University, Purdue University at Indianapolis). Unlike high school, I loved going to college. I was going part-time and working full-time at RCA, and if the class I was taking was somewhat related to my job, and I had a C average or above, RCA would pay for the class. I made the dean's list on several occasions. That was much better than being on the Assistant Principal's shit list in high school!

Tom at his desk at RCA, late '70s

When I declared my degree major I had to present my high school transcript. At that point, I had taken twenty-four credit hours at the university and was doing very well academically. As I thought, my counselor told me if the university had seen that transcript when I started, he doubted that I would have been allowed to register. My job was doing fantastic and my education was going well. I was working fifty to sixty hours a week, taking one or two classes per semester, and traveling for work an average of three days a week. Then five years later, along came another daughter. Life was wonderful! All the working and studying kept my mind occupied and Vietnam was no longer in the forefront.

When the Vietnam Veterans Memorial was dedicated in November 1982, a friend and I took off on the spur of the moment and went to Washington, D.C. to attend. We had no information on what was going on or what time it was going to happen so we just followed the crowds. After checking into a motel, we drove into D.C. to see if we could get any info and get the lay of the land. Seems like every place we went, the crowd had just left so we got only bits and pieces of info.

Finally, around 1:00 A.M. we went back to our motel for a few hours of sleep.

The next morning, we managed to find a place to park near the parade route and got some video of the parade. We watched as thousands of Vietnam vets marched down the street to the cheers of the folks along the parade route, mostly their friends, family, and other Vietnam vets. We still weren't respected or accepted by most of American society! We grabbed some lunch and made our way to the Memorial. There were so many people there, and we were so far from the Wall, all we could see was the Honor Guard standing on top of the Wall and a few inches of the top of the Wall itself. We couldn't even hear the speakers over the noise of the crowd. We finally gave up and went for a tour of the other monuments around Washington. We went back to the Memorial every few hours to see if we could get close to it. Finally, around 11:00 P.M. we got to get close enough to it to put our hands on it. We walked up and down the Wall amazed at all the names that were engraved on it. I racked my mind to remember the names of guys I knew who were killed so I could try to find their names. After years of trying to bury my thoughts and memories of Vietnam, I realized that I had managed to bury more than I ever wanted to.

When the American POWs were released from North Vietnam I felt that at last America could put this chapter of history behind us. I remember watching television as the POWs were finally returned from North Vietnam. I watched the screen looking for someone but not knowing who. I do not know why, but I felt that I had to see the faces of each man as he walked off the plane and onto free land. I rushed home each night to watch the news and became upset if I missed any of the homecomings. Then the issue of the MIAs came to light. There were lots of movies portraying what life must have been like for those men. Still today I am haunted by the fate of those listed as Missing in Action. I remember when our battalion had a man come up missing. The troops had returned to the NDP after a long day of beating the bush. Someone noticed that one of the guys was missing. The NDP was searched but he was not found. As night fell, helicopters with searchlights and loudspeakers were deployed. They were urging him to stay put and they would find him in the morning. Daybreak came and the search around the perimeter started but no trace of him was ever found. To this day I don't know what became of him. Hell, I don't even remember his name!

As the years rolled by, I buried myself in raising a family, work, and school. The days started early and finished late. Many days I was at work by 6:30 A.M. and didn't get home until after 10:00 P.M. or I was on the road making business trips. When I did get home, I was exhausted. There was not enough of my mind left at the end of the day for random thoughts, so Vietnam was pushed way back.

As I moved up the corporate ladder I found myself having less work to do, more time for myself, and more time to let my mind wander. My last job left me with lots of time during the day and my evenings were completely free. I didn't have to challenge myself to do what I was being paid to do. Shortly after I was hired into that position the company made a

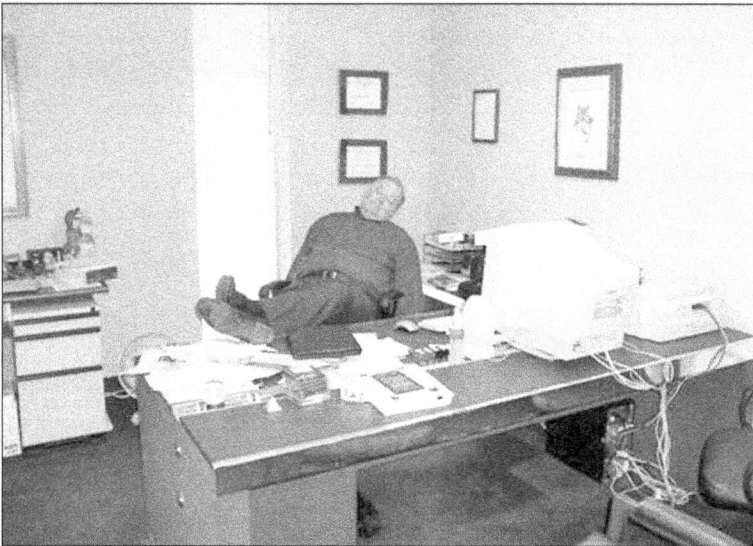

Goofing off at work, 2005

strategic change in direction and for the next six years, it was a challenge to make myself look busy and do something useful for the company. For the first time in forty-something years, my mind had lots of time to wander, and the thoughts from over forty years ago began to creep back in.

My nephew was on his last deployment to Afghanistan. And I was having flashbacks of my time in Vietnam. I wanted so badly for him to be home, safe, and to go hunting and fishing with him again. I started having serious flashbacks, not sleeping, and seeing shadow people. That is when I sought help from the local Vet Center and started to understand PTSD. The most valuable thing I learned was to stop pushing those thoughts back, but to get them out and deal with them head-on. At first, it wasn't an easy thing to do but, with the help of two very good counselors, I learned to fight my demons.

CHAPTER 26

MY RETURN TO VIETNAM

In September 2013, I made a return trip to Vietnam. It was something I had thought about for many years. At one of our division reunions, I picked up a flyer that said, "EVER THOUGHT ABOUT GOING BACK?" I took the flyer home and it set on my desk for six months before I decided to make a call to the tour company. After talking to the guy on the other end of the phone, my mind was made up and I started the paperwork for the return trip. At some point, I decided to start capturing my thoughts about what I was about to do. I am placing those thoughts here just as I had written them. I also kept a diary during the trip and took over 1300 pictures to document the trip.

Here are my thoughts, both before and during the trip:

VIETNAM EXPERIENCE PART II

MAY 15, 2013

As I continue to prepare for my return trip to Vietnam I am beginning to wonder, not only what this trip has in store for me, but what my expectations of the trip are. It has been forty-six years since I first stepped foot on Vietnamese soil, but this time, I expect it to be much different, but not sure exactly how much different. In February 1967, I was only nineteen years old when I was taken to this faraway place. I was full of expectations, anticipations, and fears. Expectations and anticipations of what it was going to be like going into combat, spending time in this backward country, and associating with the people of Vietnam. And most importantly the fears of fighting for my life and how I would react to being in combat. Would I freeze or would I do what I was trained to do without thinking and without fear?

This trip will be very different. I still have the expectations, anticipations, and a small amount of fear. Fear being the least of my concerns during this trip. But still, fear! How will I react to being back in the land where I faced the fear of imminent death or mutilation? Of being taken captive, and living in the horrid conditions of being a prisoner, of people I and my fellow soldiers had tried our damnedest to kill and eliminate from the face of the earth?

Listening to Bobby Gentry singing "Ode to Billy Joe" on the radio. The first time I heard it was on R&R from Vietnam. Brings back lots of feelings. Right after that, they played "The Red Baron." Just before going to 'Nam' one of the guys in AIT brought that record and a small record player back to Fort Polk and played that song over and over. Since that was the only entertainment we had in the evenings, we began to really like that song and danced around the barracks to it.

MAY 26, 2013

As I continue my preparations for this trip I thought it a good idea to eat at a Vietnamese restaurant. I have avoided these places for many years and wanted nothing to do with the food from Vietnam. I went to Lubbock last Tuesday, May 21st, and decided to try to get into the Saigon Cafe once again. On my first attempt, I found the cafe closed. On this trip it was open. I met Alfredo Garcia at the cafe. Al will be joining me on the trip to Vietnam. He was also stationed in Lai Khe in late '67 to early '68.

There was a large picture menu on the wall with pictures and descriptions of each dish they served in the cafe. It took what seemed to be a long time to select which dish I wanted to try. I had the flat rice noodles with chicken and shrimp. It was "just OK." The noodles were nothing to write home about. The chicken was good and both shrimp were good. They asked if I wanted mild, medium, or spicy, and I selected medium. Mistake! My lips and tongue were burning for some time after I ate.

If this is anything like the food is going to be in Vietnam, it is going to be a very long two weeks.

JUNE 1, 2013

For the past three days, I have been going through all the printed material I have concerning operations and battles I was involved in during my time in Vietnam. So far, the only absolute locations I have found are for operation Paul Bunyan. I have located that area on Google Maps and you can tell that the area of the jungle we cleared has been put to good use as farmland.

JUNE 3, 2013

I have been spending some time trying to locate information on the 18th Surgical Hospital unit that was stationed in Lai Khe for a while. One of the guys, Alfredo Garcia, I will be traveling with in September was a member of that unit, and our times in Lai Khe overlapped by a few months. Al doesn't remember a lot about Lai Khe for several reasons but I think mostly because he was only there for a few months before the unit was moved to the de-militarized zone (DMZ). I hope to be able to find some info for Al before the trip. We will work with the Vietnam Battlefield Tours guide to make sure we can spend some time in Lai Khe. Al and I may make a second trip to the area during our free day in Saigon to locate some of the Vietnamese we knew while serving there.

JUNE 15, 2013

Thanks to a book I borrowed from the Vet Center in Midland, TX, my research for locations of interest to me in Vietnam has ended. I found six-digit map coordinates for all the locations I wanted to visit:

- The Battle of Prek Klok II
- The Heart Shaped Woods - Operation Paul Bunyan
- The October 17th ambush site of 2nd /28th
- Location of Lorraine I, next to the old church being used to store weapons and ammo by the VC, in preparation for the '68 Tet Offensive
- Location of Lorraine II, 2nd /2nd location on October 17, 1967, and where SP4 Harry Carl Sarsfield, C Company, 2nd /2nd was KIA.

The only other possible site of interest to me was the NDP where we were located on Jan 14, 1968. I have only a very general idea of the location of that NDP. No big deal if I don't get back to that one, but it is one of my stressors.

JULY 4, 2013

Further preparations for Vietnam continue. Last week I had lunch in Lubbock with Alfredo Garcia at the Saigon Cafe. I took a little more time with the menu this time and the food selection was a little better, especially the egg rolls.

I pulled out the copies of the "Duty Officer's Log and Command Summary" reports that Larry Grzwynski gave me many years ago and started a thorough reading of them. I found lots of info on the Battle of Prek Klok II, including what was going on during the days preceding the battle and the move back to Lai Khe in the days after the battle. I plotted some of that information against the location of the Prek Klok II airstrip that I found in an Air Force "After Action Report." It helped confirm that I have the correct location for the airstrip.

I also found reports for Operation Paul Bunyan in the Ong Dong Jungle. A visit to this location has become more important since the revelation that this may have been the location where Joe Lupo was killed on August 26, 1967. I have a couple more people to call to try to confirm that location.

I also found the reports for the time we used the radar and searchlights to flank the battalion while they traveled across land on foot to surround a suspect VC village.

JULY 26, 2013

Well, my research is complete for now. Next week I travel to Jacksonville, Florida for the Big Red One (BRO) reunion. I will be spending some time with John Adams and we will discuss more details for the trip.

I have located the general area where Joe Lupo was killed in August '67. I have talked to several people who were in the area when he was killed but none of them can tell me which Fire Support Base (FSB) he was at when he hit the mine. The one person who could most likely tell me is LTC John Pelton and I cannot get him on the phone.

AUGUST 20, 2013

I took a road trip to Tucson, Arizona last weekend to pick up a camper trailer and bring it back to Hobbs. I was not driving so it was the first time in many years that I got to enjoy the view. After we had driven through the Guadalupe Mountains, and the terrain started to level off, I spotted something off in the distance that brought back uneasy feelings. Way out there, all by itself, was a small mountain that looked like the Black Virgin Mountain in Vietnam. As I gazed at it, I noticed that I was getting very uncomfortable inside and it made me wonder how I might handle the trip to Vietnam. I know there have been massive changes in Vietnam but some of the landmarks are still going to be there and they can't do much to change those. We shall see!

AUGUST 28, 2013

Nine days and a wake-up and I will be on the plane headed to Vietnam. Twelve hours from LAX to Taipei, a couple of hours layover and another three hours to Saigon. I am really starting to look forward to this trip.

SEPTEMBER 4, 2013

Well, I am getting damned close to making this trip. Things keep going wrong around the house and, with my health, that looks like they could get in the way but these have been minor interruptions. Getting the camper set up for Nana has been the biggest problem to overcome but it looks like those problems have settled down and most of the things left to do are minor and can wait until I get back. The latest problem to raise its ugly head was a broken water pipe outside the garage. I dug it out last night and rolled out of bed at 5:30 A.M. to go outside and get it replaced this morning before I went for my haircut. So far it is holding fine and the ladies can rest assured the water problem will not get worse while I am gone.

Most of the health issues have been resolved. My legs were swollen for over a week and I found that was in some way related to NSAID drugs like Ibuprofen so I stopped taking them for a while and the swelling went down. Then there was the constant pain in my knees that made it difficult to get around and very difficult to climb stairs. A couple of shots of cortisone in the knees last week, and now, most of that pain has been resolved with only a few glitches in my left knee. Hopefully, a little rest will take care of that and I will be good to go.

People keep asking me why I am returning to Vietnam. The latest question was asked last night during photography class. The teacher asked me what I hoped to gain from the trip and he asked it in front of the class, so there were twelve other people waiting for my answer. I really don't have a specific reason for going other than this is something that I have wanted to do for the past ten to fifteen years, so I am doing it. I hope to get some closure on the war being over but that certainly is not the only reason for the trip. I sometimes joke that I am going to visit my other children, but the truth is, I have no children in Vietnam. Never have! So, part of the adventure will be to find out what is stirring inside me, to once again, take me to the other side of the world. I can hardly wait to find out. Whatever *it* is, I will face *it* head-on and give *it* my best shot.

SEPTEMBER 7, 2013

Well, this morning the journey begins. This writing finds me full of excitement for what lies ahead during the next two weeks. I will leave Hobbs around 7:00 A.M. and drive to El Paso,

Texas and catch a flight to Los Angeles, California. This part of the journey mimics the one taken in January 1967 when my Uncle Charles and brother-in-law Gene drove me to El Paso to catch that big bird with the "Golden" tail. At that time, I flew to Los Angeles, had a long layover, then on to Oakland and a bus ride to the Oakland Army Terminal, to spend a couple of days processing, then on to Vietnam with stops in Hawaii and Manila. On that trip we arrived in Saigon around 4 A.M. and got off that airplane, full of fear of the unknown, and ready to start dodging bullets at any time. Thanks to our wonderful instructors at Fort Polk, we just knew the action would start the minute we got off the plane. As we were flying in over the coast of Vietnam, we could see battle action going on in places across the countryside, but it was too far away to be a real concern. I am sure I won't see anything like that on this trip!

The drive to El Paso was good. I stopped in the Guadalupes and took a few pictures and stretched my legs. Really enjoyed the drive. I am now on the flight to Los Angeles and listening to a little music while I read my camera instruction manual. Hope to get some great shots in Vietnam, so, I want to be able to operate the camera to give me the best pictures.

SEPTEMBER 8–10, 2013

We flew from Los Angeles to Saigon. Since we crossed the International Dateline, we lost a day during our flight. We arrived in Saigon around noon on Tuesday, September 10th and started our tour. Our first stop was the War Remnants Museum. Outside the building were many pieces of American equipment, that were left behind during the American pullout. Inside the museum, there are three floors dedicated to the "American War." Much of it is, in my opinion, propaganda, but then again, the people who build the museums get to tell the story the way they want to. From there we went to the Presidential Palace, which was left exactly the way it was when the North Vietnamese tanks crashed through the gates in April 1975 and ended the war. The tour of the Palace was very interesting, especially since everything inside the Palace, and the President's offices, were exactly as they were found by the Communists in 1975. From the Palace, it was on to Notre Dame Cathedral and Saigon's main Post Office. The Post Office is one of the oldest standing buildings in Saigon. After taking lots of pictures and buying a few souvenirs, we went to the hotel to get checked in and freshen up for dinner.

SEPTEMBER 11, 2013

Today we traveled to My Tho on the northern edge of the Mekong Delta. We took a water taxi to Coconut Island and toured a honey factory and a coconut candy factory. We rode horse carts on back streets and then small boats through very narrow canals. I envisioned this was how the VC moved men and equipment during the war. We visited the former site of the 9th Infantry Division Headquarters which has been replaced by a very large soccer stadium.

SEPTEMBER 12, 2013

Today has been one hell of a day for me. We left the hotel in Saigon and headed North, going through Phu Loi. I spent some time operating out of the Phu Loi base camp. In '67-'68 it was a great place to go, because it was an aviation base and they had lots of food and drink that we never had at Lai Khe. I managed to snap a few pictures of the old Phu Loi base which is now a Vietnamese Army base. We couldn't stop and take pictures but the bus would slow to a crawl and the guide, Mr. Phi, would say, "Get ready to take your pictures. Take now. Take now."

We left Phu Loi and headed for Highway 13, affectionately known as "Thunder Road." We called it that because of all the land mines the VC planted in the road at night. To avoid losing more vehicles and men, the road had to be swept every morning before traffic could use the road. Sometimes that worked, and sometimes it didn't. We continued up Thunder Road to Lai Khe which is the base camp I was stationed at but didn't get to see much of.

I took pictures from 1967 of two of the girls who did our laundry hoping against all odds of finding them. Well, the

Former ARVN soldier and Tom on Lai Khe airstrip, September 2013

odds were better than I thought. Mr. Phi talked to a shop owner, showed her the pictures and, low and behold, she knew Minh Nguyet's son, Mr. Hung. The woman took off with the picture on her motorbike to show the picture to Minh's son. He recognized the picture as his mother and invited us to come to his house and talk with him. Mr. Phi and I walked to the son's house and talked with him. He told us that Minh is now living in the United States with her Amerasian son. He is going to talk to her and send Mr. Phi her address which he will forward to me.

We then went in search of the old airfield and while driving down Highway 13 in Lai Khe, I spotted what looked like pavement off to the East side of the road. As we were backing up I saw a woman in a shop pointing in the direction of the airfield. She knew what this group of Americans was looking for. The whole group got off the bus and walked over to what was left of the runway. While we were there, an old man (59) came over on a motorbike and started talking to Mr. Phi. He had worked with the Americans during the war doing odd jobs. He was later drafted into the ARVN Army and lost his leg in '74 to machine gun fire. He said he would help us locate the sites of my barracks and the 18th Surgical Hospital where Al Garcia was stationed for a while. Our American tour guide, Dave Macedonia, had a different idea of how to locate the areas by going to the local market and finding some old women to talk with. They are generally the ones who remember where things were and who people are. While driving to the marketplace I spotted what I thought the possible site of the barracks. We stopped the bus and Mr. Phi, Dave Macedonia, Al Garcia, David Madrid, and I took a walk to look for the sites. As soon as I turned the corner I knew where my barracks had been located. Al and David went down a different road looking for the 18th Surgical Hospital location. We both found what we were looking for. Another win for the day.

We left Lai Khe and drove south to Ben Cat so I could take a few pictures of the streets and shops I had photographed in 1967. Although the buildings had been improved greatly, the area still looked the same. I took my pictures and we all went to a local cafe to eat the sack lunches we had bought on the way out of Saigon. After lunch, we headed up Highway 240 to locate the FSB Lorraine II where SP4 Harry Carl Sarsfield, C-2/2 was killed on Oct 17, 1967. With the help of Dave's GPS and some map coordinates I had researched, we found the site. Although several farms have been built in the area, once I saw the area I knew we were there. We all got off the bus and I passed out some flowers we had bought on the way out of Saigon. I told the story of the day Carl was killed and we had a moment of silence followed by a prayer provided by one of the Vets on the tour. I stuck my flower in the ground and all the other guys did the same. While we were there we were joined by two Vietnamese men from nearby. They had a conversation with Mr. Phi but I did not ask what was said.

We left there and drove to Tay Ninh City where we will spend the night.

This was a fantastic day! I will say that I felt some highs and lows today, but, mostly highs with a forty-six-year-old weight lifted off my shoulders.

I expect more of the same over the next two days as we visit the site of my first major battle in Vietnam and the site where Joe Lupo was killed. More flowers will be laid and more prayers will be said.

SEPTEMBER 13, 2013

Another home run this morning!

We left Tay Ninh City and drove north past Nui Ba Dinh and on up to the site of the Prek Klok II Battle on March 10, 1967. There were tremendous changes in the area and a town has sprung up on the site of our former NDP. We stopped the bus and studied the maps, GPS, and iPad info, and decided we were very close to the site of the runway. We got out of the bus and walked a few blocks and found a very straight dirt road that Dave and I thought was the runway. A man came along on a motorbike and told us we were standing on the runway. We did further exploration further west of the road and found nothing that looked like it could have been the runway. We walked back to take pictures and were greeted by three women who also confirmed that we were in the right place. I could tell by the soil that this was the runway. The US always used laterite as a base for roads and runways. It is a heavy clay soil with small crushed rocks in it and compacts into a very hard surface. Then PSP (Perforated Steel Planking) was laid over it to make the final landing surface.

I told Mr. Phi that there was a mass grave to the southwest of the airfield. He again asked the locals and found a man who knew where the site was. He took us there and told us it had been excavated many years ago, and the 197 bodies were removed and sent to another location for proper burial. I chose that site for the memorial service for the three Americans and 197 Vietnamese who lost their lives in that battle. Again, we had a very nice ceremony and laid some flowers.

Yet another monkey has been taken off my back!

Two more to go . . .

We then went back to Tay Ninh City to visit the Cao Da Temple to observe the noon worship service and have lunch at a restaurant owned by a former Viet Cong soldier. Mrs. Ngoc Tuyet is a very famous soldier in Vietnam and a very gracious hostess. We had the best meal of any so far in Vietnam. It was a seven-course meal (very small courses) and then took pictures with her in her uniform. It was nice to exchange greetings with a person who, in 1967, would have been trying to kill me, and I her.

After lunch, we visited the Coa Da Temple and watched part of the noon worship service. It was very interesting to experience. The Coa Da Temple is made up of four different religions, all living and worshiping in peace and harmony—Buddhism, Muslim, Confucius, and Taoism. Each group wears a different color showing their religion. The people dressed in white signify followers of the Coa Da.

We then drove to the Cu Chi tunnels and watched a government propaganda film made in 1967. The film was boring, it was hotter than hell, and there was no breeze, so I napped off and on like several others in the group. We then toured the tunnels but I did not go in any of them—mostly because of my knees and partly because I just didn't have a need to see it.

Now we are headed back to Saigon and will be there for the next three nights before heading for the Central Highlands. On Sunday we have a free day in Saigon and John Adams and I are going to rent a car to drive to the October 17th ambush site where the 2/28 Black Lions were decimated.

SEPTEMBER 14, 2013

Another great day!

We left Saigon and headed northeast to Di An, site of the 1st Infantry Division Headquarters and later the Rear Detachment. Like several other former Army and Air Force bases we have visited, the Vietnamese Government had built an Army post on that location. We couldn't stop for pictures, so we just slowed down so that anyone wanting to take pictures could do so without getting off the bus.

Then it was on to Tan Uyen and the Ong Dong Jungle to look for the general area where Joe Lupo was killed on August

26, 1967. We located a good spot to lay the flowers and had a short memorial service for Joe. On our way back to the bus, we were approached by two ladies who were talking to me in Vietnamese. Mr. Phi had gone ahead of us and I had no idea what the women were saying. I finally figured out that they wanted to have their picture made with the Americans. As has been the case in all the places we have been, the people are very friendly and were all smiles and trying their best to communicate with us.

We then traveled back in the direction of Saigon to visit Bien Hoa Airfield and Long Binh, the location of the 90th Replacement Depot. Again, both have been converted into Vietnamese Army bases and taking pictures was very difficult. We had a memorial service for friends of the two guys from Ohio, and for Dave Macedonia's brother-in-law. After the service, some of us were trying to stand on a park bench to get a view of the old American runway. A man came over and was talking with Mr. Phi and when he found who we were and what we were doing, he invited us into his home which had a very nice balcony overlooking the airfield. We went in and up four stories to his rooftop patio where we had a beautiful view of the airfield.

We drove back into Saigon for lunch at a very famous noodle restaurant, according to Mr. Phi. I will say it was good but I would sure like to have some Mexican food for a change or a cheeseburger from Nip-a-Hut.

We went by an orphanage to drop off some clothing and other supplies that were donated by folks on the tour. The kids were all gone to the park so we didn't get to visit with them.

Then back to the hotel early to rest up for dinner.

SEPTEMBER 15, 2013

Today was a free day in Saigon for the group. Most of the group slept in and went to various places around Saigon, but Dave Macedonia, John Adams, Mr. Phi, and I got a private car and driver and took a road trip to several locations that were of interest to John and me. John served with the 1st Battalion, 2nd Infantry and I served with the 2nd Battalion, 2nd Infantry. We were often on joint operations but in separate locations. We were both on Operation Shenandoah II in October '67 when the 2/28 ran into a regiment-sized ambush and was decimated. A visit to this site was the last point of importance for me, but, on this day, John had two other points that he wanted to visit.

First stop was to place a plaque in memory of 3 KIAs from 1/2. LTC Mortimer O'Connor, 1LT Robert Lulia, and SFC Alejandro De Jesus, all KIA on April 1, 1968.

The next stop was to place a plaque to all those 2/28 soldiers killed and missing on the Battle of Ong Thanh on October 17, 1967. On that day my unit was located at FSB Lorraine II, just south of the 2/28. I have very vivid memories of the calls coming across the radio as the battle started. They were calling for artillery, air strikes, and reinforcements. Later that day is when Carl Sarsfield was KIA on our perimeter. When the VC broke contact with 2/28 they moved south and passed near our FSB and Sarsfield and his group were just far enough away from our FSB that they made light contact with the fleeing VC.

The next stop was to place a plaque for a group of six men from 1/2 who were KIA on October 4, 1967.

We finally made our way out of the huge rubber plantation and back onto Thunder Road, Highway 13, to head south back to Saigon. Along the way, we stopped at an open-air restaurant for lunch. What luck we had when we randomly picked that place for lunch. It sat right in front of a small lake and there was a fishing contest going on. The banks around the lake were lined with people fishing for catfish. We watched several large catfish being pulled out of the lake, and someone would bring them to the judge for check-in, and take them back to the lake and release them. The food was very good.

On the way back to Saigon we stopped on the north side of Lai Khe so I could get some photos of the place we used to operate the radar from and go swimming. Everything had changed, even the shape of the stream.

Then back to Saigon for dinner and spending the evening repacking for our very early flight to Da Lat.

SEPTEMBER 16, 2013

This morning we left the hotel at 6 A.M. for an early flight from Saigon to Da Lat. Da Lat is a mountain resort town that was originally built up by the French in the 1920s. They built many resorts in the area because it is much cooler than any other place in Vietnam. It is a beautiful area.

Once we arrived we were met by our Vietnamese guide, Mr. Phuoc. He lives in Hue and came down to Da Lat to meet us with a much smaller tour bus than we have had for the last week. The group is down to six people now; the rest went north to join the other group that came over.

Once on the bus, our first stop was a Buddhist Temple called Truc Lam Da Lat. This was an absolutely beautiful place. You will just have to look at the pictures to appreciate the beauty.

We then went to the palace of the last King of Vietnam. In 1946 the King moved to France and was replaced by a President, who continued to use the palace as a summer resort. At the end of the tour, I was made an Honorary King.

Upon leaving the palace we tried to visit several Lam villages, which turned out to be just shops in other areas of town. All the villages and shops were closed so we retired to the hotel for a nap before dinner.

During the evening I heard drums and other instruments playing. Vietnam is approaching the mid-autumn festival, also known as the Full Moon Festival. People dressed in a lion costume dance around the street to drum music. They go from house to house or business to business. The owners give them money to drive out the bad spirits and leave good spirits.

SEPTEMBER 17, 2013

We left Da Lat and drove to the top of the pass and then down the long twisting road to the west side of the mountains. Da Lat is in the southern part of the Central Highlands.

We drove to Cam Ranh Bay, the home for the 22 Replacement Battalion, 14th Aerial Port, and the 6th Convalescent Hospital. There was very little left of these facilities except concrete slabs and a few buildings. We did locate one barracks building in the area of the 22nd Replacement Battalion. It won't be long before that is gone to make way for a resort area. We saw two new high-rise buildings that are under construction in the area.

The 14th Aerial Port is still being used as a commercial airport.

During our visit, we were paid a visit by four Vietnamese soldiers who were checking us out. One of them was a captain who would not allow his photo to be taken until Dave offered to give him $10 to buy beer for him and his buddies.

This is the area that about eighty percent of the Army Replacement Troops were processed into and out of the country, so it was of some significance to several of the guys on the tour.

After much time roaming around and taking photos, we boarded the bus for the ride to Nha Trang. What a beautiful ride up and down mountains along the coastline. We arrived in Nha Trang around 5:30 P.M. and had two hours before we met for dinner at a local "Smoked Beef" restaurant. And I mean dive. But the food was pretty good. We had two small charcoal grills on our table and put small pieces of marinated beef on there and cooked it. Of course, there were rice and vegetables to go with it along with a bowl of soup. We are eating lots of soup and rice.

The hotel in Nha Trang was fantastic, best so far. We all wanted to stay for a couple of days, but the next morning it was back on the bus for more adventures in Vietnam.

SEPTEMBER 18, 2013 – NHA TRANG TO QUI NHON

After breakfast, we drove north to Qui Nhon. Along the way, we passed Tuy Hoa Airbase. This was one of the largest American airfields in Vietnam during the war. We couldn't go on the base, but we stopped alongside the base for a look and to take some photos. We could see the US revetments with Vietnamese Air Force jets sitting in them.

Across the street, there were farmers working to turn rice straw. I went over and watched so I could get a better understanding of what they were doing.

We were traveling through this area during the major rice harvest so we saw how the rice was cut and separated. Some of it was done by machines and some was still being harvested by hand. There were machines that drove through the rice patties cutting and bundling the rice and another machine that took those bundles and separated the rice grains from the straw.

If it was being done manually, the farmers were using sickles to cut the stalks, it was carried up the bank to the road and someone else was pounding it against the pavement to get the rice kernels off the stalks.

The rice is then spread on the road, and the stalks are spread alongside the road for drying. The rice is raked out in thin layers with rakes or by foot. Sometimes they get the rice a little too far out into the road and trucks, bikes, and motorcycles run over it. No one seems to get upset they just rake it again and go about their business. As I have said before, the people are very warm and friendly.

Driving through the mountains we saw several places where water from hoses was squirting high in the air. The water is from artesian springs and has a natural pressure. All these places are truck and car washes. Squirting water in the air from several hoses is very effective advertising because you can see it well before you get to it.

When we got back down to the coast we began to go through fishing villages. There are boats of all sizes in the bay, including the small round boats. They look like baskets woven from reeds and then tarred on the bottom. There is one paddle in the boat. I have no idea how they make it go where they want it to go, but the guide told us they were very stable in the ocean and rode over the waves with no problem.

We had lunch at another roadside cafe. When I went to the WC (toilet) there were chickens roaming all around the back of the cafe. When you order something with chicken in it at this place it is fresh. I had fried noodles with vegetables and chicken, but, after what I saw and thought about, I just couldn't eat the chicken.

Then it was back into the mountains and on to Quin Nhon for the evening.

We had a wonderful meal that was fixed, sort of, Italian style with Vietnamese flair. But it was good.

SEPTEMBER 19, 2013

This morning we visited two sites of the Cham ruins. The Cham people ruled what is today's Vietnam from the 3rd to the 15th centuries. The buildings were built of locally-made brick and put together without using any cement. The mortar between the bricks was made of coconut oil and grass. To this day they have not been able to duplicate that formula. The first temple was in the city of Quin Nhon. Although the grounds were well-maintained, nothing has been done to the temple. It is amazing the detail that is found in this work. We then went to the "Bang It" Temple in the Village of Ba Di. This ruin was three buildings located on top of a hill with a steep climb. What the hell, I am only going to see this place once, so I made the climb to the first building and took photos from there. Big mistake! My knees were really talking to me by the time I made it back down.

I did meet a twenty-five-year-old Vietnamese man at the first temple who was riding his bike, no motor, just peddles, from Saigon to Hanoi. He was taking a month off work to make this trip. He would travel for a day and then spend the next day exploring the area he had stopped in. He would repeat that routine until he reached Hanoi. He has been on the road for ten days.

Once we all got back on the bus we headed west on Highway 19 towards An Khe. We drove up the long winding hill, through the An Khe Pass, and over the An Khe Summit. A little after noon we arrived in An Khe to pick up an additional

Vietnamese guide, Mr. Cham, and to have lunch. The lunch was in a large hall that was also used for wedding receptions.

There was a group of Vietnamese men there and when I walked by them after lunch, one of them got up to shake my hand. I didn't know if he was eating something hot, or if he was crying, but there were tears in his eyes. He just kept shaking my hand and talking to me in Vietnamese. Neither of our guides was around so I have no idea what he was saying, but I think he was a veteran of the American War, as they call it over here. A second man got up to shake my hand and started talking to me. Just then Mr. Cham came over and interrupted what he was saying. It turns out that he was an officer in the North Vietnamese Army when Saigon fell in 1974. He said, "We were enemies at one time but now we can be friends." He is so right. Yet another load off my shoulders.

This is the first group of men who were smiling and willing to talk to us Americans. The entire group stood to shake my hand before I left. What a great lunch stop . . .

An Khe was the headquarters for the 1st Cavalry Division. We managed to find the base camp for the headquarters and found some of the barracks still standing and in relatively good shape.

Now a little history about our new guide, Mr. Cham, a member of the Montagnard tribe.

His dad was a military man and served with the ARVN Army. When Mr. Cham was seventeen years old he moved to Ann Arbor, Michigan to attend the University of Michigan. He came back to Vietnam in 1974 just before the fall of Saigon. In 1975 he was arrested because he had a college education from the US and spent eight months in "reeducation camp" in Saigon. He was kept in a Conex container with a couple of holes cut in it for ventilation. At one point he was put in solitary confinement in a hole in the ground with no light coming in. He said when he got out of that he couldn't stand to open his eyes because there was too much light. When he was released from Saigon he was given a certificate and told to move to Pleiku and give that certificate to the local police station. When he did that, he was arrested and sent to prison for another seven months with no reason given. He holds no animosity against the Vietnamese government. As he said, "That is all behind us now."

After lunch, we left town across the An Khe bridge and continued west through the Mang Yang Pass. This is where the French Mobile Group 100 was ambushed and annihilated on June 24, 1954. We stopped at the memorial and listened to explanations by Mr. Cham.

We arrived in Pleiku at around 3:30 P.M. and will spend the next two nights here.

SEPTEMBER 20, 2013

This morning we traveled north on Highway 14 to Kontum. Kontum was one of the major objectives of the three-prong 1972 Easter Offensive attacks by the NVA (DMZ in I-Corps; Kontum in II-Corps; and An Loc in Ill-Corps). The road was under construction for most of the trip so the going was slow and rough.

In Kontum, we will visit the Kontum Wooden church and the Vinh Son Montagnard Orphanage. The Catholic church was unique because very few churches in Vietnam are built of wood. Most are constructed with cement or bricks. We toured the church and the grounds then went to the orphanage located behind the church. The church alone was certainly not worth the trip to Kontum, but the orphanage was wonderful. There were 197 kids in the orphanage, on the day we visited, and as we strolled around we had a chance to interact with many of them. We were taken to the dining hall where we were served hot green tea and the head nun and Mr. Cham told us about the operation of the orphanage, including a breakdown of the number of kids by age, sex, and disability. After that, we went into the nursery section of the orphanage and got there during lunchtime. About a dozen kids were lined up, sitting on the floor (as is the tradition in Vietnam), having a bowl of some sort of corn chowder. These kids were in the eighteen to twenty-four-month range. Most of them were very friendly and curious about all these tall (and wide) people they were looking at. One little guy was very forward and toddled over to Dave and put his arms up. Dave picked him up and they were having a ball making faces at each other. Another one came over to me and wanted to be picked up so I obliged him. For a little kid, he was heavy. I might add here that the kids we met were very well taken care of including clothes and food. They all appeared to be happy and healthy which is a very good thing in Vietnam. Many of the peasant kids in the farming communities were very slim.

We left the little ones and went to a room with eight to ten kids in the two to four-year-old range. They had been fed, were ready to play and attacked our group with screams and laughter. One little guy wanted me to pick him up, so, he could get to the toys hanging on clotheslines above our heads. There were stuffed animals hanging everywhere. When I put him down to leave he didn't want to let me go. As I started down the stairs to leave there were three or four kids pulling at my shirt and pants. I was delighted to see how well they were taken care of, but it pulled at my heartstrings to have to leave them. This made the long bumpy trip worth the time. I will put this orphanage on my Christmas shopping list.

We drove to a Montagnard Communal Center that was made of wood and grass and was on stilts. Mr. Cham told us a lot about the Montagnard tribe and it was very interesting.

Some of us climbed the steps to see the inside of the Communal Center. Absolutely nothing was up there except bees. Dave got about a dozen stings on his back and arms, Dean got one on his hand, and Mr. Phouc got one on his top lip. This morning his lip is huge. Dean was fine and I haven't talked to Dave yet.

We had lunch at another small cafe that only served noodle soup. I wanted fried rice with shaved beef so Mr. Phouc went next door to a different cafe and ordered it for me. They brought it over and it was very good. That will be the day when you see a waitress from Chili's delivering a meal to a customer in Applebee's.

We drove the long bumpy road back to Pleiku and had an afternoon of rest and relaxation.

Dave mentioned pretzels as we were getting off the bus and that just stuck in my mind. I went to the lobby to see if I could find some in the bar or restaurant. The closest they could come was to offer to make me some French fries. The manager at the hotel then sent me to a shop across the street because he knew they would have them. No one in the shop spoke English but lots of customers were curious about this tall American in the shop. I tried to communicate but nothing was working, so I just looked around to see what I could find. I found lots of cookies but no salty snacks. The shop owner pulled something off the top shelf that turned out to be a supplement of some kind. Then she brought me some Ensure. I gave up and went back to the hotel, propped my legs up, and took a nap.

Dinner was at a local cafe where we had a semi-private dining room with only one cat roaming around. It also served as the place where the dirty dishes were stacked in bins. I ordered fried noodles with shrimp and vegetables and it was very good. I decided it was time to give the chopsticks a try and ended up eating the entire meal with chopsticks, except for the soup.

SEPTEMBER 21, 2013 – PLEIKU TO SAIGON

We took a mid-morning flight to Saigon. While we were sitting in the waiting area at the gate a young Vietnamese woman walked over to me, motioned for me to take her baby, and pointed at the WC. I took the kid and she headed for the bathroom. You would never find that in the US unless the woman is trying to dump her kid.

Pleiku airport is the site of one of the first attacks on American Forces in Vietnam. Several American aircraft were destroyed. The old American runways are still in use and several of the old buildings are still visible. There is a hill nearby that has buildings and guard towers, that was most likely the site of an American radar and communications installation.

Got back to Saigon around 3 P.M. I walked to the large shopping mall and bought some camera accessories then went back to the hotel for a nap and shower before our farewell dinner.

Dinner was very good and most people told stories about their experiences in Vietnam. The dinner was a long affair, but we got to sleep in before the noon flight from Saigon to Taipei.

A LITTLE ABOUT SAIGON

Ten million people live in Saigon. Another three million people come into Saigon every day to work. On any given day there are nine million motor scooters on the streets of Saigon. We witnessed one accident during our two-week stay. Our bus backed into a parked motor scooter, neither the bike or the driver were hurt, but, it required a payoff to the owner of the bike.

The motor scooters are the major mode of transportation in Vietnam. The law allows two riders per scooter unless they are family; it is not unusual to see a family of four on one scooter. I tried to get photos of that, but, it was hard to do from the bus. Helmets are required for all passengers on a scooter except for infants.

Saigon, September 2013

The motor scooters are also used to haul all sorts of things, even baskets of pigs going to market. I saw two riders on one scooter carrying a ten-foot ladder. The balance and maneuvering of the scooters is something to see.

SEPTEMBER 22, 2013 – SAIGON TO TAIPEI TO LOS ANGELES

We headed to the airport at 10:30 A.M. to start our journey home. The flight from Saigon to Taipei was uneventful. We managed to miss the typhoon that came across southern Taiwan and into Hong Kong. We had a short layover in Taipei and boarded the flight to Los Angeles. I can't say enough good about EVA airlines. All four flights were customer-focused and very comfortable. EVA is a Taiwan-based airline.

On the way from Taipei, we gained a day by crossing the International Dateline, so we all got a little younger on that flight. We arrived in Los Angeles around 3:30 P.M. and made our way through US Customs. What an ordeal! We went through four different lines before we made it outside and onto the bus to the hotel.

Five people took flights home and the rest of us stayed the night and flew out on Monday. Sunday night, several of us went to dinner at a Mexican restaurant and discussed the trip. Everyone agreed that we had a great time.

CHAPTER 27

CONCLUSION

When I started writing this book I did not know what to expect. As I wrote, I began to relive old experiences, which in turn caused more and more memories to come back. As I wrote the first few chapters about my life as a young boy, growing up in New Mexico, I began to feel good about the life experiences I had during that time

As I moved into the chapters about preparing to go to Vietnam "that thing inside me" started to come out. I now realize that the thing inside me that needed out was the denial I have lived with since the beginning of my trip to Vietnam. The first occasion of this thing getting out happened as I wrote Chapter 8 "Oakland Bound or California Here I Come." The emotions came back so hard and so quickly I had to stop writing until I could recompose myself. I found myself reliving the fear I had of going to Vietnam and dying in that far away land. I had never allowed myself to face the realities of what might have been while I was in the Oakland Army Terminal waiting to be put on a plane for Vietnam. As I wrote about those experiences the fear that I had repressed for so many years came out and I allowed myself to finally deal with those emotions. Emotions that I could not, or would not, have shown twenty-seven years earlier. Although it was painful, the overall effect was one of accepting my past and starting the healing process. That thing inside me is coming out and I feel it is going to make me a better person by forcing me to deal with the feelings, the emotions, and the memories.

The writing of this book has drawn out for many years, all part of the healing process. I have said several times during the writing that I had reached an understanding and had moved forward with my life, but, I know now that it was not until my nephew, Marc, came back from his third trip to the sandbox of Iraq and Afghanistan, that things started to really fall into place for me.

In March 2003, Marc came to me and wanted to talk about what the Army was like. His dad was a career Navy man so Marc had grown up in the Navy. He had graduated high school and needed to do something meaningful with his life and at that time college was not an option. He and his dad had decided that he should go into the service. He knew what the Navy was like and decided he wanted to go into the Army and get into electronics. His dad made him promise to talk with me before he joined. He spent the weekend with me and I went over, in detail, what my two years in the Army had been like. I told him stories and showed him pictures of my time in Vietnam. I made sure he had a good understanding of what he would be getting himself into. I explained Basic Training and Advanced Individual Training. I told him that every person who went into the Army had to take eight weeks of Basic Infantry Training before they went for their selected Advanced Individual Training. I guess I spent a little too much time on the Infantry part of my discussion. He left at noon on Sunday to go meet with the Army Recruiter and when I talked to him on Monday he proudly told me that he had signed up for Infantry Training. He said I had told him that every soldier's basic job in the Army was Infantry and if that is what he was going to end up doing he wanted to make sure he had the best training. So, a few months later he was off to Fort Benning, Georgia for his Basic and Advanced Infantry Training. When we went down for his graduation from AIT he told all his friends and his drill instructors that his uncle, a Vietnam Vet, was coming for the graduation. For the first time since getting out of the service, I was treated with honor and respect by all the military personnel that I met.

After graduation, Marc was assigned to the 2nd Battalion, 22nd Infantry Regiment, 10th Mountain Division. After about six months at Fort Drum, New York, he was off for his first tour in Iraq. Back stateside for a few months and then back to Afghanistan. Another short stay in the States and then back to Afghanistan for his third tour in the sandbox.

The whole time Marc was deployed I had my eyes glued to the evening news. I saw Congress acting the same way they did during the Vietnam War. Instead of presenting a united front to support the troops, they were bickering about who started the war and why the American Government was involved. I wanted to go over there and protect my nephew but realized it would probably be him who was protecting me. I was just too damned old to be a soldier again and I felt so helpless that I couldn't be there for him.

When he came home from his last deployment I was talking to him on the phone. "It's a beautiful sunny day at Fort Drum," he told me. "But every time a car drives by, I feel myself getting uneasy and wanting to go hide in the barracks."

"You have PTSD", I told him. "Get out of the Army and come back to Indy and I will go with you to the Vet Center and get you some help. You have done enough for your country."

That is when it struck me that I also needed help coping with PTSD, something I had never considered until that time. Well, Marc got out of the Army and moved to California and I decided to take my own advice and went to the Vet Center to seek counseling. I was diagnosed with severe PTSD and have spent the past twelve years with several different counselors and PTSD groups. One of the counselors helped me get at my demons and put many of the bad thoughts and nightmares behind me. The counselors didn't cure my PTSD, but they helped me understand it and cope with it and I will always be grateful for that. A trip to Vietnam in September 2013 helped me lay down lots of baggage, most of which I didn't even realize I was carrying.

In 2014 I helped a young, homeless, unemployed, Marine veteran of the war in Afghanistan, identify some of his demons and get him into the treatment he so deserved. At last contact he was doing fine, working three jobs and living in a home he had purchased. I am so proud of him!

During the writing of this book, I have discussed the feeling that something needed to get out. I have touched on my life before, during, and after my service in Vietnam. The feelings of family and friends before Vietnam and the subtle, but frequent rejection I felt when I returned from Vietnam. Even from family, including my parents and my wife. I recently found out that my mother had a fear that I may have done unspeakable things in Vietnam, thanks mostly to the liberal news media, and their effort, to often create fantastic stories from untruths, all for the sake of selling a few more papers, or, getting their ratings up on the evening news. My wife even told me she was made to feel ashamed of me because I had participated in the Vietnam War. Although the words were not spoken until years later, the feelings were there and I could see them in people's eyes and feel them, especially from friends and other people who were supposed to love and support me. Those feelings contributed to me burying my thoughts and memories of Vietnam in a deep place, which contributed to the rise of PTSD inside me to fill that void. Thanks in part to two very good Vet Center counselors I learned what PTSD was and was not, and how to cope with *it*. I am now able to openly discuss my time in Vietnam with other veterans who have similar experiences. I am once again able to take control of my PTSD and my life. There are many Vietnam veterans, as well as veterans of other wars, who refuse to talk about their experiences and thoughts and as a result are seen by many people, who just don't get it, as being that crazy vet who came back from the war a changed man. Lord knows he must have done something horrible because he just doesn't fit the pattern society accepts as normal anymore. And the vets buy into that because they don't fit the pattern of "the old normal" anymore. And for good reason! Our behaviors are the product of all the things we experience in our lives, both good and bad. When a person experiences a war, they are adding thoughts and memories that don't fit in with what our pampered society considers as normal activities. Therefore, the Veteran's "new normal" is moved to a different place on the scale, and if we as veterans, try to compare our new normal to the normal our non-military friends have, we are different, and not necessarily in a bad way. I am sure we have all looked at our extended families and wondered, why can't we be a normal family? Take a minute and ask yourself, "What does a truly normal family look and act like?" So much for normal!

When I was working with that young Marine vet, I tried to explain to him that there was a new normal in town. The "normal" that is accepted by most of society is based on the normal everyday experiences of people who have not experienced war. Once a person has been put in a new situation, those experiences establish a new normal. It doesn't mean we are "weird" or "evil," it just means we have experienced things that others haven't, and therefore they cannot understand. Once we veterans learn to accept and understand our new normal we can begin to move on with our lives. Yes, we still startle easier than many people, but who cares. That reflex helped keep us alive during our "truly formative years in Vietnam." Be thankful you had those experiences and can react faster and more efficiently than "normal" people.

Another important lesson I have learned from counseling is to allow myself to grieve for my losses. Even though some of them happened fifty years ago, on the other side of the world, they still need to be addressed. While in Vietnam we didn't have the luxury of being able to take the time to say good-bye to our buddies or think about the tragic events we experienced. We just had to bury it inside and move on. Even after the war, when I experienced the death of friends and family, I did not grieve. I held it in, bit the bullet, and moved on. As men, we are often taught that we are not allowed to cry because it is a sign of weakness. After a session with one of my counselors, talking about this very thing, he convinced me that it was OK to let it out. If crying helped me to get past it, let the tears roll until there were no more. Like many of you, I have what the VA refers to as "stressors" usually associated with a date when bad things happened. Those dates would often sneak up on me and I found myself feeling depressed and moody. I'm sure now that other people around me noticed it more than I did. For almost fifty years I became irritable and depressed on certain dates, without even thinking about what day it was. One day I was in the shower when it hit me and I realized what day it was. I sat down at the end of the bed and let it out until there were no more tears, and I felt better. When the next stressor date came around I realized that I felt less tension and depression than normal. Over time I put much of that behind me and often don't realize, I have gone past a stressor date until it has passed. This technique, along with my return to Vietnam in 2013, has helped me move on with my life. Don't think for a minute I have forgotten those things that took place many years ago, they have just become easier to live with.

TOM COPELAND

I grew up in a very close-knit family in the desert of southeastern New Mexico. After graduation from high school, I moved to Indiana where I started my working career. I was drafted into the US Army in August 1966 and served in Vietnam with the 2nd Battalion, 2nd Infantry Regiment, 1st Infantry Division from February 1967- January 1968.

After my release from the Army, I returned to working and raising a family. I showed some very early signs of PTSD, but as years progressed IT began to creep into my life and become more prevalent. Over the years, IT took ITs toll, but with counseling, and a return trip to Vietnam in 2013, I have managed to put many of my issues behind me, and/ or, learned to control them.

I was married in 1966, one month before my deployment to Vietnam. I have two daughters and three grandsons from that marriage. I was divorced in 2008 due to, among other things, the effects of PTSD on the marriage.

I moved back to New Mexico in 2008, and on Veteran's Day, 2010, I married a lady I knew in High School.

My working career spanned 42 years and five companies with jobs ranging from a cleaner/sweeper at a Consumer Electronics Company to President of a Medical Device Manufacturer.

I have two degrees from Purdue University in Organizational Management.

I am now retired and living in Oklahoma with my second wife and enjoying my hobbies, including fishing and carving.

www.ingramcontent.com/pod-product-compliance
Lightning Source LLC
Chambersburg PA
CBHW021402090426
42742CB00009B/963